DIVERSITY MANAGEMENT AND DISCRIMINATION

Research in Migration and Ethnic Relations Series

Series Editor:
Maykel Verkuyten, ERCOMER
Utrecht University

The Research in Migration and Ethnic Relations series has been at the forefront of research in the field for ten years. The series has built an international reputation for cutting edge theoretical work, for comparative research especially on Europe and for nationally-based studies with broader relevance to international issues. Published in association with the European Research Centre on Migration and Ethnic Relations (ERCOMER), Utrecht University, it draws contributions from the best international scholars in the field, offering an interdisciplinary perspective on some of the key issues of the contemporary world.

Other titles in the series

Moving Lives
Narratives of Nation and Migration among Europeans in Post-War Britain
Kathy Burrell
ISBN 0 7546 4574 6

Immigrant Women and Feminism in Italy
Wendy Pojmann
ISBN 0 7546 4674 2

Cities and Labour Immigration
Comparing Policy Responses in Amsterdam, Paris, Rome and Tel Aviv
Michael Alexander
ISBN 0 7546 4722 6

**EUROPEAN RESEARCH CENTRE
ON MIGRATION & ETHNIC RELATIONS**

Diversity Management and Discrimination
Immigrants and Ethnic Minorities in the EU

JOHN WRENCH
Unit for Health Promotion Research,
University of Southern Denmark, Esbjerg

ASHGATE

Published by
Ashgate Publishing Limited
Gower House
Croft Road
Aldershot
Hampshire GU11 3HR
England

Ashgate Publishing Company
Suite 420
101 Cherry Street
Burlington, VT 05401-4405
USA

Ashgate website: http://www.ashgate.com

British Library Cataloguing in Publication Data
Wrench, John
    Diversity management and discrimination : immigrants and
    ethnic minorities in the EU. - (Research in migration and
    ethnic relations series)
    1. Diversity in the workplace 2. Diversity in the workplace
    - European Union countries 3. Immigrants - Employment
    4. Minorities - Employment 5. Marginality, Social
    I. Title
    331.1'143

Library of Congress Cataloging-in-Publication Data
Wrench, John.
    Diversity management and discrimination : immigrants and ethnic minorities in the EU
    / by John Wrench.
       p. cm. -- (Research in migration and ethnic relations series)
    Includes bibliographical references and index.
    ISBN 978-0-7546-4890-1
    1. Diversity in the workplace--Europe. 2. Personnel management--Europe. 3. Race
discrimination--Europe--Prevention. I. Title.

    HF5549.5.M5W74 2007
    658.30089--dc22

2006037658

ISBN 13: 978-0-7546-4890-1

Printed and bound in Great Britain by Antony Rowe Ltd, Chippenham, Wiltshire.

Contents

Acknowledgements

The idea for this book first came in March 1998 when I spent a brief period as *Directeur d'études associée* at the Ecole des Hautes Etudes en Sciences Sociales, in Paris. It was here that I was able to make use of the opportunity to read and reflect on the characteristically French approach to issues of immigration and ethnic diversity and its implications for what French colleagues no doubt regarded as the very 'Anglo-Saxon' strategy of diversity management. Later, at the University of Southern Denmark, I introduced questions of European comparison into the Diversity Management courses for the *cand. negot.* and *cand. merc.* programmes in Odense and Kolding and the International Studies programme in Esbjerg. In 2000 I received a commission from the Swedish National Institute for Working Life to write a report on issues around the development of diversity management in a European context. The report, entitled 'Diversity Management, Discrimination and Ethnic Minorities in Europe: Clarifications, Critiques and Research Agendas' was presented as an occasional paper of the Centre for Ethnic and Urban Studies, Norrköping, in 2002, and served as the foundation for this book.

In 2003 I was given leave of absence by the University of Southern Denmark to join the European Monitoring Centre on Racism and Xenophobia (EUMC), an agency of the European Commission, in Vienna, where I became acquainted at first hand with the rich data and information on issues of racism and discrimination gathered since 2000 by the EUMC's National Focal Points located in each of the member states of the EU. This publicly available material, which is increasingly recognised as an invaluable and unique source of comparative data by scholars of racism, integration and migration in Europe, enabled me to add to the book new dimensions of European themes and examples.

I would like to extend my thanks to Professor Michel Wieviorka at CADIS, Ecole des Hautes Etudes en Sciences Sociales, for providing the original opportunity for the kernel of the idea of this book to be planted, to the students at the University of Southern Denmark who endured the first diversity management course taught in a Danish university and provided so readily their ideas and feedback, to Professor Carl-Ulrik Schierup and his colleagues at the Centre for Ethnic and Urban Studies, Norrköping, (University of Linköping) for commissioning the original occasional paper and providing invaluable feedback on the first draft, and to the diversity management practitioners in various EU countries who willingly gave their time to be interviewed for this book. Finally, I would like to thank my wife, Sheila, for her constant support, her copy-editing skills and her helpful suggestions.

I would like to emphasise that the views expressed in this book are mine alone, and not those of the European Monitoring Centre on Racism and Xenophobia.

John Wrench

List of Abbreviations

AA	Affirmative Action
ABVV	Algemeen Belgisch Vakverbond (Belgian General Federation of Labour)
ACLVB	Algemene Centrale der Liberale Vakbonden Van België (Belgian Liberal Trade-Union)
ACV	Algemeen Christelijk Vakverbond (Belgian Christian Trade-Union)
BDA	Bundesvereinigung der Deutschen Arbeitgeberverbände (Confederation of German Employers' Associations)
CEOOR	Centre for Equal Opportunities and Opposition to Racism (Belgium)
CRE	Commission for Racial Equality
DGB	Deutscher Gewerkschaftsbund (German trade union umbrella organisation)
EBTp	European Business Test Panel
ECRI	European Commission against Racism and Intolerance
EEO	Equal Employment Opportunity
ENAR	European Network Against Racism
EUMC	European Monitoring Centre on Racism and Xenophobia
EU 15	The 15 member states of the European Union before the enlargement in 2004
ILO	International Labour Office
NGO	Non-Governmental Organisation
OFCCP	Office of Federal Contract Compliance Programs (US Department of Labor)
SME	Small and Medium-sized Enterprise
TUC	Trades Union Congress (UK)

Chapter 1

Introducing the Issues

In response to the growing demographic diversity of the European workforce, both private and public sector organisations have turned to specific policies to facilitate the recruitment, inclusion and retention of employees of diverse backgrounds. Diversity management as a business practice was first seriously discussed in a European context at the beginning of the 1990s. Interest in the practice slowly grew, and ten years later examples of companies operating diversity management policies could be found in a steadily increasing number of EU countries. In this context, the aim of the book is to clarify concepts relevant to the practice, and provide contextual information in order to better understand the development of diversity management in European countries.[1]

Chapter 1 sets out the parameters of the book and looks at various definitions of diversity management. Chapter 2 looks at the origins of diversity management and the factors which have provided a stimulus to its development in the US, and provides examples of the kinds of activities which take place under the heading of diversity management in US companies. Chapter 3 looks at the background context for the development of diversity management in Europe, and Chapter 4 considers the variables of European difference which may have implications for the form, content and dissemination of diversity management practice. Chapter 5 presents an overview of critiques of diversity management that have been advanced by both academics and equality activists. Chapter 6 explores the relationship of diversity management to the specific issue of combating racial discrimination in the sphere of employment. Chapter 7 concludes with some observations on both positive and negative developments in Europe which may be relevant to diversity management, and highlights a number of issues and trends that should be monitored by those concerned with racial and ethnic equality in employment.

The parameters of this book must be made clear from the outset. Firstly, whilst the practice of diversity management encompasses a wide range of variables of 'difference', this book approaches diversity management from the point of view of those who are interested primarily in the dimensions of 'race' and ethnic origin, and the related issues of equality and employment integration.

Secondly, there is no attempt to provide an overview of existing North American and European diversity management literature, and nor will there be an attempt to provide a picture of the current state of diversity management practice in Europe. The former would be an immense task, and the latter a research project for the future. Instead the book draws on selected key sources of information with the aim

---

1   The focus of this book is on the countries within the European Union, and therefore the terms 'Europe' or 'European countries' is employed only in this restricted sense.

of highlighting some of the relevant issues for those who wish to observe or research the development of diversity management in the European context.

Thirdly, the book makes no attempt to address the sorts of questions which have been asked in many other studies of diversity in organisations, such as 'what are the effects of demographic diversity on a workforce's creativity or productivity?', or 'how can managing diversity techniques contribute to organisational goals?'. Instead, this book is guided by a number of more specific interests:

- What can diversity management ideology and practice demonstrate to those who are concerned with issues of ethnic inequality and racial discrimination, and with the inclusion and exclusion of immigrants and their descendants in the labour market, in organisations and in European societies?
- Is diversity management to be seen as a valuable new way of mainstreaming anti-discrimination measures, or alternatively, should it be regarded with scepticism as being a 'soft option', intrinsically weak on combating racism and discrimination in employment?
- Will the development of diversity management in EU member states follow a relatively uniform trajectory because of commonly experienced demographic, economic and market pressures, or will the historical, cultural, political and institutional differences which exist amongst EU countries, (and between the EU and the US) have a determining impact on the adoption, content and mode of operation of this particular management practice in Europe?

It should be noted that this book is more relevant to *intranational* diversity management, which refers to managing a diverse workforce within a single national organisational context, rather than cross-national diversity management which refers to managing a workforce in different countries (see Mor Barak 2005: 209).

Methodology

This book draws heavily on literature searches on diversity management, both published and on the Internet. Most of the literature was American, with other sources coming from Canada, Europe, Australia and New Zealand. Where possible, use has been made of already existing surveys and overviews of practices and literature relating to diversity management.

The book has not sought to provide new primary data on the development of diversity management in Europe, but has drawn on existing evidence of the development of diversity management in organisations across EU member states, often from material published by the European Commission. In particular, much information has been taken from the data gathered annually by the European Monitoring Centre on Racism and Xenophobia (EUMC) and made available in its publications and on its website. The aim has been to provide an analysis of secondary data which can help to clarify the issues for future research and policy-making. As part of this process the book modifies or creates from new a number of typologies covering discrimination, anti-discrimination and organisational activities. These serve as points of reference for understanding and classifying practices, and as bases for comparison of these activities between national contexts within Europe. These typologies may then be refined and modified by further research.

Further material has come from interviews carried out since 2000 with people who have direct experience of diversity management and related issues, who were able to provide an insight into diversity management developments in their respective EU countries. Eight of these were formal semi-structured interviews lasting between one and two hours. The eight respondents came from four countries: Denmark, the Netherlands, Sweden and the UK. Most acted for at least part of their time as diversity management consultants, and the others worked in NGOs or agencies concerned with the promotion of ethnic equality and/or diversity management at work. A great deal of further information was gleaned from more informal interviews carried out with participants in conferences or workshops on the subject of diversity management or related issues of employment equity strategies between 2000–2006 in Belgium, Canada, Denmark, Italy, the Netherlands, Spain, Sweden, Switzerland, the UK and the US.

What is diversity management?

Diversity management is the latest development in a sequence of strategies which have aimed to get excluded minorities better represented in employment. However, diversity management is said to be characteristically different from previous employment equity approaches directed at under-represented minority ethnic groups, such as equal opportunity and affirmative action approaches, in a number of ways. For one thing, its rationale is primarily one of improving organisational competitiveness and efficiency, driven by business purpose and market advantage. In relation to this it emphasises the necessity of recognising cultural differences between groups of employees, and making practical allowances for such differences in organisational policies. The idea is that encouraging an environment of cultural diversity where peoples' differences are valued enables people to work to their full potential in a richer, more creative and more productive work environment. An advantage of diversity management is said to be its more positive approach, rather than the negative one of simply avoiding transgressions of anti-discrimination laws. It is said to avoid some of the 'backlash' problems associated with affirmative action, as unlike previous equality strategies, diversity management is not seen as a policy solely directed towards the interests of excluded or under-represented minorities. Rather it is seen as an inclusive policy, and one which therefore encompasses the interests of all employees, including white males.

A multiplicity of metaphors

Advocates of diversity management have a tendency to draw on metaphors to explain its advantages, and these metaphors are different from those of previous approaches. For example, the earlier analogy of the 'melting pot', with its overtones of assimilation and 'sameness', is replaced with that of the 'mosaic', where 'Differences come together to create a whole organisation in much the same way that single pieces of a mosaic come together to create a pattern. Each piece is acknowledged, accepted and has a place in the whole structure' (Kandola and Fullerton 1998: 8). An American food company's commitment to diversity used the metaphor 'A stellar meal requires contrasting and complementing textures and tastes.' Other examples are 'A winning sports team depends on the different talents of its members. A first-class orchestra needs many varied instruments. And a successful business team requires a variety of thought, energy and insight to attain and maintain a competitive edge' (*HR Magazine* November 1998). The American diversity writer and consultant R. R. Thomas chooses a 'jar of jelly beans' to illustrate what he wants to say about diversity:

> .... consider a jar of red jelly beans and assume that you will add some green and purple jelly beans. I suggest that diversity ... is represented by the resulting mixture of red green and purple jelly beans. When faced with a collection of diverse jelly beans, most managers have not been addressing diversity but, instead, have been addressing how to handle the last jelly beans added to the mixture ... (Thomas 1996, quoted in Mor Barak 2005: 209).

More recently, another American diversity author, Michàlle Mor Barak, suggests:

> In depicting diverse management, I propose an image from the art world – the painter's palette. Like colors, when people are forced to blend and give up their unique characteristics, the result is a dull gray. Allowed to display their true colors, they shine brightly and together create an inspiring work of art (Mor Barak 2005: 292).

Metaphors such as 'the salad bowl' and 'the patchwork quilt', like 'the mosaic', are all part of what one American critic called the 'celebratory and harmonious imagery' which aim to convey how the whole is 'enriched by the differences of its component parts' (Kersten 2000: 242).

However, the creativity exhibited in the generation of diversity metaphors masks a frequent conceptual slackness around the use of the concept of diversity management. There is some genuine confusion about what the term covers, particularly in the European context, where the term 'diversity policy' is in some cases simply employed to refer to any policy at all which relates to the employment of immigrants and minorities. Yet some commentators insist that a 'diversity policy' must contain something different from already existing practices of combating discrimination in the organisation. There must be a 'managing for diversity' element which is more than furthering equal access to employment opportunity, and certainly more than just employing immigrants. It should refer to particular techniques of actively managing the diverse mix of people within the organisation in ways to contribute to organisational efficiency or business advantage (Wise 2000: 3).

Something else which causes confusion is the way that the word 'diversity' is sometimes used in practice. Instead of referring simply to the demographic mixture of people within an organisation, the term 'diversity' is becoming a shorthand for the practice of dealing with this mixture, i.e. the approach itself. This can be seen in the replies to a 1997 US survey where respondents were asked to define diversity in their organisations. Replies included 'Diversity today is valuing the differences among people and ensuring that the work environment is representative of the variety of people that represents our country', 'Diversity fosters an environment where all employees have the opportunity to reach their full potential' or 'Diversity is the full utilization of all the talents and energies of all our people' (Wentling and Palma-Rivas 1997c). In each of these cases it would have been more accurate to replace the word 'diversity' by a term such as 'diversity management' or 'managing for diversity'. In this book the conceptual distinction will be maintained between 'diversity' as the condition of heterogeneity, and 'diversity management' as the management of that condition.

There is also wide variety in what are seen as the important dimensions of diversity that should form the focus of organisational policies. Some prioritise the main 'primary' dimensions – sex, age, 'race' and ethnicity – whereas others see the term as encompassing every dimension of human difference within the organisation. For a more focused definition of diversity we can turn to Mor Barak (2005: 132). She defines workforce diversity as the division of the workforce into categories of distinction that have a perceived commonality within a given cultural or national context and that have an impact on potentially harmful or beneficial employment outcomes such as job opportunities, treatment in the workplace and promotion prospects, irrespective of job-related skills and qualifications. Such a definition emphasises the consequences of the distinction categories, which for Mor Barak overcomes the problem of over-broad definitions of diversity that include 'benign and inconsequential' characteristics in their diversity categories. (For further discussion of this problem see Chapter 5.)

As stated earlier, this book approaches the topic primarily from the point of view of the 'racial'/ethnic dimension, which includes a consideration of the implications of locating 'ethnic equality' practices within such an all-encompassing policy.

The ethnic dimension

Although the practice of diversity management in the US is by definition multi-dimensional, the dimension of 'race'/ethnicity is generally near the top in priority for managers in organisations. This is also the 'angle' which has perhaps most stimulated interest in the subject by practitioners and politicians in Europe. European governments are becoming increasingly concerned about issues of the social inclusion and exclusion of immigrants and ethnic minorities[2] within their borders, and the important role that integration into employment plays in this. The communities established by post-World War II labour migrants in western European countries have long been over-represented in long-term unemployment or in poorly paid, insecure and generally less desirable work. There has been a tradition of media, politicians and public discourse emphasising 'supply-side' factors in this

---

2 The phrase 'immigrants and ethnic minorities' is used to cover visible minorities in Europe who are potentially subject to social exclusion and discrimination. In practice, this will cover mainly the post-World War II immigrants and refugees from outside Europe, and their descendants who often, but not always, have citizenship rights in an EU member state. However, some ethnic minority groups subject to discrimination may also come from within Europe, such as the indigenous Roma.

– immigrants are seen as having a weak command of the local language, or as having a poor educational history and fewer qualifications and skills. 'Integration policies' therefore try to reduce these supply-side disadvantages by encouraging immigrants to take language courses, improve their education and attend vocational training courses, or perhaps courses in the host country's culture and institutions. However, in recent years in Europe there has been an increasingly vocalised concern that this emphasis is flawed. Certainly an education and training approach can be relevant for many newly arrived immigrants and refugees, or in cases where economic restructuring and organisational changes have put new demands on longer-established immigrant workers (Wrench 1998: 37). However, they are less relevant for many long-settled migrants and their children. The problems faced by these groups are less easily explained by supply-side arguments. Even with fluency of language and parity in educational attainment, members of minority ethnic groups suffer labour market exclusion and marginalisation in comparison with their majority national peers. Here, demand–side factors are more important in constraining the employment opportunities of ethnic minorities in Europe (Zegers de Beijl 2000). One of these demand-side factors is 'racial' or ethnic discrimination. Indeed, according to the Annual Reports presented by the European Monitoring Centre on Racism and Xenophobia (EUMC), since 2002, the labour market and the workplace are frequently the main areas of complaints of discrimination by immigrants and members of ethnic and religious minorities living in EU member states.

Once the focus of attention shifts to the structures of societies itself – the institutions, laws and organisational practices – then diversity management becomes relevant. If part of the problem in the past has been direct or indirect organisational practices of exclusion, then diversity management represents an inclusive alternative.

Definitions of diversity management

At this stage it might be useful to consider a selection of definitions of diversity management set out by practitioners and academics. These have been taken primarily from two American sources, (Wentling and Palma-Rivas 1997c; the Society for Human Resource Management) and one British (Kandola and Fullerton 1998). An American survey asked business practitioners to define 'diversity' within their organisations and describe how they had arrived at the definition. One common factor was that all defined the term in its broad sense, so that it could embrace everyone in the organisation. As one respondent put it, it is 'an initiative that benefits everyone' rather than a particular group of people. Others talked about 'having an inclusive environment in which everyone is valued and respected', 'the full utilisation of resources', or bringing 'our employees, customers, vendors, communities, and other associates together in a way that it has a positive impact on our performance.' One respondent said 'We are a global organization and, therefore, we needed a global perspective; so we defined diversity very broadly in order to tap into all the creativity and potential that diversity brings' (Wentling and Palma-Rivas 1997c: 19).

The Society for Human Resource Management provides examples of how several leading American companies approach the subject. For example, Texas

Instruments (TI) states that their 'effectiveness at using the talents of people of different backgrounds, experiences and perspectives is key to our competitive edge ... Diversity is a core TI value; valuing diversity in our workforce is at the core of the TI Values Statement ... Every TI'er must work to create an environment that promotes diversity ... Each TI business will develop diversity strategies and measurements ...'. Similarly Harvard Pilgrim Healthcare state that they are 'committed to increasing the diversity of staff at all levels while paying special attention to improving the representation of women and minorities in key positions; to creating an inclusive, respectful and equitable environment; to serving our diverse members with culturally sensitive services, and to changing the organizational culture through leadership, policies and practices.' [3]

Kandola and Fullerton (1998: 7) collected a sample of definitions from a range of written sources, and these provided definitions consistent with those above, such as 'Understanding that there are differences among employees and that these differences, if properly managed, are an asset to work being done more efficiently and effectively' (Bartz et al. 1990: 321) or '...creating an environment that taps the potential of all employees without any group being advantaged by irrelevant classification or accident of birth' (Hammond and Kleiner 1992: 7). Another example is:

> People are different from one another in many ways – in age, gender, education, values, physical ability, mental capacity, personality, experiences, culture and the way each approaches work. Gaining the diversity advantage means acknowledging, understanding, and appreciating these differences and developing a workplace that enhances their value – by being flexible enough to meet needs and preferences – to create a motivating and rewarding environment (Jamieson and O'Mara 1991: 3–4.)

Kandola and Fullerton then come up with their own definition of diversity management:

> The basic concept of managing diversity accepts that the workforce consists of a diverse population of people. The diversity consists of visible and non-visible differences which will include factors such as sex, age, background, race, disability, personality and workstyle. It is founded on the premise that harnessing these differences will create a productive environment in which everybody feels valued, where their talents are being fully utilised and in which organisational goals are met (Kandola and Fullerton 1998: 8).

Primary and secondary dimensions

There are differences as to which particular dimensions of diversity are perceived as important. Wentling and Palma-Rivas state that in the US some people use narrow definitions which reflect American equal employment opportunity law, and define diversity in terms of race, gender, ethnicity, age, national origin, religion, and disability, whereas others simply define diversity as 'All the ways in which we differ' (Hayles 1996: 105). Perhaps the most useful distinction they quote is that by Griggs

---

3   'How should my organization define diversity?' SHRM, www.shrm.org/diversity/definingdiversity.htm

(1995), who classifies diversity into primary and secondary dimensions. Primary dimensions of diversity defined as are those human differences that are inborn and/or that exert an important impact on early socialisation and have an ongoing impact throughout life. The six primary dimensions include

(1) age
(2) ethnicity
(3) gender
(4) physical abilities/qualities
(5) race
(6) sexual/affectional orientation.

According to Griggs, these primary dimensions cannot be changed; they shape our basic self-image and have great influence on how we view the world.

Secondary dimensions of diversity are defined as those that can be changed, and these might include educational background, income, marital status, parental status, religious beliefs, and so on (Wentling and Palma-Rivas 1997a: 2). Others have added 'physical appearance' to the first group and 'language' and 'lifestyle' to the second; some call the first group 'biological' dimensions and the second group 'experiential'.

Wise (2000: 3) warns that although practitioners think of human diversity mainly in terms of the primary dimensions of race, sex, and ethnicity, it should be noted that in the scholarly literature, heterogeneity and diversity often embrace a very broad spectrum of individual differences. Many of the academic studies of the effects of human heterogeneity on work-group and organisational performance have used the broad secondary dimensions of diversity, and it should be recognised that many key assumptions about diversity in the workplace are in fact drawn from research where diversity is very broadly defined. (This point is addressed further in Chapter 5.)

Differences from other approaches

If managing diversity is to be differentiated from previous assimilation approaches and the 'melting pot' metaphor, it is also to be differentiated from a conventional 'equal opportunities' approach too. American and British authors set out what they see as the main distinctions between diversity management and other employment equity approaches common in their respective countries. For the American case, Wentling and Palma-Rivas summarise the differences between American affirmative action/equal employment opportunity (EEO/AA) approaches and managing diversity approaches, as first set out by Fernandez (1993). What marks out a managing diversity approach as different includes the fact that top management play a leading role, it is a strategic element of the business plan, it is linked to managerial performance evaluations and rewards, it is long term, and it is inclusive of all employees, rather than simply focusing on excluded groups.

The American author Kersten (2000) summarises what she sees as the core features which make diversity management different and distinctive compared to previous approaches to tackling discrimination. She identifies four main aspects to this. Firstly, diversity management advocates a systemic transformation of the organisation as opposed to the singular emphasis on recruitment/selection that was characteristic of the older methods. Most commonly, there will be a 'diversity audit' of the company culture and its workforce statistics, then there will be a 'diversity plan' over several years that includes taskforces, extensive training programmes that focus on teambuilding, cooperation and mentoring, and sometimes hiring and promotion plans. 'In general, the stated aim of these diversity efforts is to change the organizational culture in such a way that it becomes an open, welcome and supportive environment for all people.'

Secondly, diversity management is also different in its rhetoric. 'Diversity is not presented as a negative, external mandate but as a positive and voluntary effort on the part of the organization'. The third difference is that diversity efforts are justified with economic rather than legal arguments. Thus, it is argued that diversity will make the organisation more competitive in the labour market, enable better recruitment, facilitate the retention of qualified employees, create higher levels of productivity, creativity and group synergy, and allow more effective management of conflict within the organisation. 'Diversity management is not seen as a goal in and of itself, to be justified through some appeal to idealistic notions of justice, equality or fairness. Rather, it is an instrumental goal designed to enhance the overall effectiveness of the business itself.'

Finally, diversity management approaches use an inclusive definition of diversity in which any and all differences are considered as part of the diversity project. As an example she quotes from the Ford Motor Company: 'Diversity in the workplace includes all differences that define each of us as unique individuals. Differences such as culture, ethnicity, race, gender, nationality, age, religion, disability, sexual orientation, education, experiences, opinions and beliefs are just some of the distinctions we each bring to the workplace. By understanding, respecting and valuing these differences, we can capitalize on the benefits that diversity brings to the Company'. By considering all people as 'equally unique', diversity management seeks to appeal to a broad audience (Kersten 2000: 242).

The British authors Kandola and Fullerton largely agree with the American writers over the main differences between diversity management and what is called in Britain an 'equal opportunities' approach, (which can include within it 'positive action' rather than US-style affirmative action). In particular, Kandola and Fullerton see managing diversity as differing from equal opportunities in its lack of reliance upon positive action. Positive action is where organisations take special initiatives to redress perceived gender or ethnic imbalances in the workforce by, for example, providing special training for women and minorities. A number of American authors argue that there is no place for such measures within diversity management – 'organisations must recruit, develop and promote on the basis of competence rather than group membership' – and Kandola and Fullerton agree that 'If managing diversity is about individuals and their contribution to an organisation rather than about groups, it is contradictory to provide training and other opportunities based solely on people's perceived group membership.' In fact, as we shall see in Chapter 5, there are some diversity management practitioners who disagree with this view.

The American writers Kelly and Dobbin (1998) set out their own interpretation of the differences between diversity management and earlier approaches. However, in their case they make a three-fold distinction between equal employment opportunities (EEO), affirmative action and diversity approaches, and add some more subtle dimensions to the scheme, such as the differences in cultural values which are implicit in the three approaches. For example, the values underlying the equal employment opportunity approach are egalitarianism and meritocracy, and those underlying the affirmative action approach are a concern to remedy past wrongs. These contrast with the values underpinning diversity management which are inclusiveness and a respect for difference. There are similarly distinct differences regarding the views of the solutions in each case. According to the EEO approach, formalisation and commitment to non-discrimination will lead to minorities' and women's advancement. For an affirmative action approach, it is targeted programmes for recruitment, mentoring, and training that will lead to minorities' and women's advancement. According to the diversity approach, it is efforts to change the organisational culture that will remove the systemic, institutional barriers blocking minorities' and women's advancement (Kelly and Dobbin 1998: 976).

Some writers further divide the 'diversity' category into two stages, distinguishing an earlier stage of 'valuing diversity' from the later stage of 'diversity management' (Thomas 1990). Valuing diversity is a stage beyond affirmative action because it involves a positive recognition of the differences among people in the organisation, valuing the contribution that each can make to the work environment. Managing diversity goes further than this by actively managing these differences in ways which contribute directly to business goals (Wise 2000: 3).

Kelly and Dobbin make it clear that their distinctions relate to differences in theory, whereas in practice there is a 'significant convergence' between the types. The same point can made regarding the distinctions made by others quoted in this section above, namely that the differences between diversity management and earlier approaches on some dimensions can be considered to have been somewhat overstated. This might reflect an academic desire to create more distinctive 'ideal types' for theoretical and conceptual clarification; on the other hand, more prosaically, it may reflect an activist's desire to distinguish it from more unpopular approaches, thereby making the work of diversity management consultants more acceptable to business. As will be seen later in this book, the difference between diversity management and earlier approaches is in practice not always clear.

The advantages of diversity management

Across the diversity management literature there can be found an ever-expanding number of case studies of private companies and public sector organisations which describe their own experiences of the benefits that diversity initiatives have provided to their organisation. The major recurring themes and stated advantages of diversity management in such case studies can be summarised below:

  • using the skills and talents of the workforce appropriately, and ensuring that recruitment and selection decisions are based on rational criteria.

- avoiding internal problems such as conflicts and misunderstandings, grievances, higher absenteeism, greater staff turnover, and damage to staff development.
- making products or services more attractive to multi-ethnic customers and clients.
- increasing creativity, innovation and problem solving through the inventiveness of diverse work teams.
- stimulating more flexible working practices through responding to the needs of a diverse workforce. This flexibility itself can enhance the creativity and efficiency of the organisation.
- accessing international markets with more success, in particular when a diverse workforce allows a company to draw on the skills or connections of employees to reach new markets.
- avoiding the costs of racial discrimination, such as damage to the organisation's image through adverse publicity, and/or the financial penalties resulting from legal cases.
- enhancing the likelihood of winning contracts in situations where national or local government authorities operate a system of 'contract compliance' regarding equality and anti-discrimination issues.
- enhancing the likelihood of winning contracts through the positive image of a diverse sales team, or winning sales from corporate clients who themselves put a high priority on the diversity policies of their suppliers or partners.
- Improving the image of the company in the eyes of potential investors who choose to invest in companies demonstrating practices of corporate social responsibility.

Whilst some diversity management advocates collectively bundle all these as universally accessible advantages, it is clear, as we see in Chapter 5, that in reality not all of these are relevant in all types of organisation and in all circumstances.

Chapter 2

Diversity Management in the USA

This chapter presents information on diversity management origin and practice in the USA, so as to provide the background for understanding developments in Europe. First, there is a consideration of the factors that have been generally seen as providing the stimulus to the growth of diversity management in the US. This is followed by a brief presentation of examples of the main constituents of diversity management practice in the US, drawing on existing surveys of the topic.

The origins of diversity management in the US

What caused the shift in thinking towards diversity management at the end of the 1980s in the US? American accounts generally agree on a similar set of factors which brought about this change. The first and key factor is usually stated to be the demographic one.

1. Demographic developments

In their reviews of the subject, Wentling and Palma-Rivas (1997a; 1997c) single out *Workforce 2000: Work and Workers for the Twenty-First Century* (Johnston and Packer 1987) as one of the most cited references in this respect. This and other reports made it clear that dramatic changes were to be expected in the composition of the US workforce over the coming decades:

> the demographic change will be away from the European-American male and more towards an increasingly diverse and segmented population. This population will include women and men of all races, ethnic backgrounds, ages, and lifestyles. It will include people of diverse sexual/affectional orientations, religious beliefs, and different physical abilities, who will need to work together effectively (Wentling and Palma-Rivas 1997a: 3).

Thus it was argued that if managers did not find some way to accommodate this change, and how to recruit, manage and retain a diverse body of employees, then the competitiveness of their organisation would suffer.

By the early 1990s, business leaders in the US were starting to sit up and take note. Wentling and Palma-Rivas quote a survey of 645 firms by the Towers Perrin & Hudson Institute (1990) which found that '74 percent of the respondents were concerned about increased diversity and, of these, about one-third felt that diversity affected their corporate strategy.' Most importantly:

This study also revealed two primary reasons for managing diversity: (1) the perception that supervisors did not know how to motivate their diverse work groups and (2) an uncertainty about how to handle the challenge of communicating with employees whose cultural backgrounds result in differing assumptions, values, and – sometimes – language skills (Wentling and Palma-Rivas 1997a: 4).

It has been pointed out that in recent years Hispanics and minority racial groups – non-Hispanic blacks, Asians (e.g. Chinese, Japanese, Koreans) and American Indians – have each grown faster than the population as a whole. Whereas in 1970 these groups represented 16 per cent of the US population, by 1998 they had reached 27 per cent, and estimates put them at almost 50 per cent of the US population by 2050 (Mendoza 2000).[1] When this is set in the context of an overall shrinking workforce and shortages of appropriately skilled labour, then the pressure on employers to attract and retain a more heterogeneous range of employees becomes even more crucial to business success. Johnston and Packer (1987) pointed out that over the coming decade, visible minorities, women and immigrants would account for 85 per cent of net new workers in the US labour force.[2] Many authors pointed out the fact that in the context of a diverse workforce, companies were penalising themselves with unnecessary and excessive recruitment and training costs when women and ethnic minorities were exhibiting far higher labour turnover rates than white males, because of an unsympathetic organisational culture and environment.

An added dimension of demographic change is the fact that young people, who are more ethnically diverse than ever, are entering the workplace at a time when the American workforce itself is ageing, throwing up new permutations of age and ethnic groups amongst co-workers.

2. The growth in minority communities as markets

As the workforce is becoming more heterogeneous, so is the domestic market becoming more ethnically diverse. The implication for businesses and service providers is that the employment of a diverse workforce and the proper management of this diversity will be increasingly necessary in order to be able to compete effectively in selling goods and services in these markets.

> Diverse customers are more complex and differ in their needs, tastes, and desires. To understand and respond properly to a diverse customer base, businesses need to make their own workforce more diverse. ..... by having employees who represent the diverse marketplace, organizations can communicate and serve diverse customers more effectively (Wentling and Palma-Rivas 1997b: 4).

---

1   Some authorities dispute this and suggest the figure for the non-white US population in 2040 will be closer to 25 per cent (Lynch 1997: 35).

2   Lynch (1997: 35–36) points out that this figure is frequently misunderstood and misquoted, and in reality means that the total number of new white male workforce entrants is more like 32.5 per cent of all the newly hired.

3. The growth in the service sector

Another common factor quoted in the growth of diversity management is the shift from a manufacturing-based economy to a service economy. The fact that the majority of jobs in the US are now in the service sector provides a stimulus in itself to diversity management practices. This is because in the service area, interpersonal skills of employees have a greater intrinsic importance, with potential direct effects on the quality of service provision, and interactions between employees and clients have a direct bearing on business success. The argument is that customers are becoming more demanding, and will reflect a wider range of preferences than in the past. There will be more variation in what constitutes 'good service', and employees need to be able to interact with and 'read' customers who are increasingly diverse, ethnically and in other ways (Kossek and Lobel 1996: 7–8). In some cases companies will feel the need to recruit staff who reflect the ethnic mix of customer groups.

4. Organisational changes

Over the past decade or so organisations have undergone changes in their structures and in their operations in ways which are said to have direct implications for diversity management. New management strategies such as Total Quality Management place importance on harnessing the creativity and experience of individual employees in achieving organisational goals. Flexible working patterns and new forms of work organisation such as team working – including self-managed teams – have new implications for employee involvement and participation (Shapiro 2000: 304). Studies have shown that organisations which fail to gain and sustain employee involvement in these circumstances can experience difficulties in achieving organisational objectives. Shapiro argues that such problems can be a result of the tendency of organisations to value, train or communicate better with some groups of employees rather than others, and a failure to recognise the various factors that will motivate diverse employees to become involved. It is argued that 'High and sustainable levels of employee involvement are dependent on creating an organisational environment that values, develops and motivates all employees' (Shapiro 2000: 305) – in other words, the proper management of diversity.

5. Globalisation and the increasing importance of foreign markets

US companies are increasingly buying companies in other parts of the world, and foreign companies are increasingly buying US companies. The North American Free Trade Agreement, the consolidation of the European Union single market, and the disintegration of the former Soviet Union have all had implications in the 1990s for the internationalisation of organisational practices in the context of new opportunities for foreign links, investments and markets. The increasingly international way that organisations operate means that companies are faced with the need to manage diversity both at home and with their global partners (Kandola and Fullerton 1998: 30). Thus American corporations need a more multicultural perspective to be able to relate to employees, suppliers and customers abroad, and must develop the appropriate human resource practices to reflect this.

The above are generally agreed in American textbooks to be the kinds of factors which help in understanding the development of diversity management in America. Two further factors were suggested by a telephone survey of twelve diversity experts from across the United States (Wentling and Palma-Rivas 1997b). These experts had been selected because of their experience on working with diversity programmes in both public and private sectors, their publication and research record in the field of diversity, and their roles as diversity consultants with corporate and public-sector clients. When asked to identify the major factors that are influencing diversity initiatives in the workplace, they generally quoted the kinds of developments set out above – demographic changes, the diverse customer base and the increasingly global marketplace, and so on, but also mentioned two more: the qualitative changes in American identity politics and the pressure of American equal employment opportunity and affirmative action (EEO/AA) programmes.

With regard to the former, it was mentioned that now, in the increasingly diverse American workforce, people are 'more comfortable being different'. In the words of the authors of the report:

> These people bring to the workplace a variety of experiences, values, cultures, physical abilities, religions, work styles, and so forth. They are no longer willing to deny their differences in order to assimilate into the organization's mainstream. They want to maintain their uniqueness and still receive the respect and support of the people they work with. They essentially want to be given the opportunity to use their talents and full potential and not have to pretend to be somebody else (Wentling and Palma-Rivas 1997b: 4).

With regard to the second mentioned factor – the pressure of American equal employment opportunity and affirmative action programmes – this is not really a reason which accounts for the specific development of diversity management as it was already a factor in existence for equal opportunity initiatives pre-dating diversity management. Nevertheless, it should be seen as a factor which plays a part in the *continuation* of diversity management. These final two factors may be significant when embarking later on the examination of the European context, as these appear to be factors which may not apply to the same extent outside of the US.

Wentling and Palma-Rivas sum up the implications for the US. The demographic changes mean that employers will be forced to compete to attract, retain, and effectively manage all available employees. Now organisations are changing their cultures and beginning to apply more emphasis to valuing and managing diversity mainly because they have a greater understanding of the significant role that diversity will play in their future competitive and organisational success (Wentling and Palma-Rivas 1997a: 4).

'Best practice' in the US diversity field

In 1997 the US Equal Employment Opportunity Commission set out what it saw as 'best practice in achieving diversity' (Mendoza 2000). The Commission convened an internal task force and published a report entitled 'Best Practices of Private Sector Employers.' This divided policies, programmes, and practices into seven major groupings:

1. Recruitment and Hiring: Here the emphasis is on affirmative recruitment programmes designed to create a diverse workforce, such as 'internships' or work experience, recruitment strategies, and education and training programmes used for hiring.
2. Promotions and Career Advancement: These initiatives are on programmes that have eliminated barriers to the advancement of diverse under-represented groups. They include mentoring, education and training for purposes of promotion, and career enhancement initiatives.
3. Terms and Conditions: Under this heading the focus is on programmes to accommodate differences such as on religion, as well as on harassment at work, pay equity, employee benefits, and family-friendly policies and practices.
4. Termination and Downsizing: Here, examples of good practice are seen as retraining and placement programmes, financial counselling or training grants and loans for employees displaced by downsizing programmes, and non-discriminatory early retirement programmes.
5. Alternative Dispute Resolution: This heading covers initiatives on 'early resolution of employment discrimination complaints and voluntary and effective alternative dispute resolution programs', including mediation and arbitration.
6. Leadership and Accountability: The focus here is on what management was saying and doing, performance appraisals, compensation incentives, and other evaluation measures.
7. Other: This category covers 'other policies, programs or practices not readily identified'. An example here is groups and networks within the organisation for women or minorities.

In the same year a survey of American employers presented examples of the kinds of initiatives that were current in multinational corporations that had diversity policies (Wentling and Palma-Rivas 1997c). For their survey Wentling and Palma-Rivas used interviews with workforce diversity managers or directors responsible for diversity initiatives in multinational corporations whose headquarters were in the state of Illinois. Eight companies were selected that were considered to be 'exemplary in their diversity efforts'. They were all Fortune 500 multinational corporations and represented the sectors of food, electronics, chemicals, petroleum and pharmaceuticals, plus one specialist retailer. The interview material was augmented by analysis of documents relating to the organisations' diversity initiatives and annual reports as well as from broader sources.

Factors which had influenced diversity policy

The study participants were asked to list the factors which had influenced diversity initiatives in their organisations. All of them identified the following factors: demographic changes, the diverse marketplace, and the need to improve productivity and remain competitive. They explained that a diverse workforce and a changing market place are related in a way that has implications for their internal practices. As one stated 'We are now starting to realize that we cannot effectively address diversity in the marketplace without also effectively addressing diversity in the workplace' (Wentling and Palma-Rivas 1997c: 21). What was noticeable in the replies of these respondents was their unquestioning assumption that diversity management was related directly to improving productivity and remaining competitive. For six out of the eight companies, globalisation was stated to be an important factor influencing diversity initiatives, as these companies now had to 'understand global markets and cultural implications of conducting business worldwide' (Wentling and Palma-Rivas 1997c: 21). One said

> We have been really proactive. We see that if we don't have the diversity we need on board and we don't value and leverage it, we are not going to be successful in the global market, because we will not be able to deal effectively with the diversity issues here and in other countries. To be successful, we have to have the global perspective (Wentling and Palma-Rivas 1997c: 22).

Three of the eight company respondents also cited legal concerns as a factor influencing their adoption of diversity initiatives, as 'implementation of effective diversity initiatives can assist in the reduction and prevention of costly lawsuits relating to race discrimination, sexual harassment, and gender discrimination lawsuits' (Wentling and Palma-Rivas 1997: 21). Half of the study participants mentioned 'the Texaco incident'. This was a $176m racial discrimination lawsuit against Texaco, which 'created awareness for these corporations regarding the negative effects of not having diversity initiatives in place'. One of the respondents stated that the President of his company 'basically said he did not want their company to be a Texaco' (Wentling and Palma-Rivas 1997c: 22).

All of the corporations stated that they had started their diversity programmes as a result of the Civil Rights Act or movement, and the necessity of complying with affirmative action requirements. This brought women and minorities into the organisations; however, they were at the lowest levels, and without any support systems – 'they were treated like outsiders.' They were not being fully utilised, and had high rates of labour turnover. This led to the second stage in the evolution of diversity initiatives, the development of support systems. The initiatives introduced by the majority of the corporations at this stage included task forces, employee networks, advisory councils, hiring consultants to develop frameworks for addressing diversity, and introducing awareness-based diversity training. Later stages included the start of articulation of the business case for diversity, a more strategic approach to diversity linked to the business plan, the involvement of upper level management, and the communication of the value of the diversity process in company newsletters or speeches. In some cases diversity accountability guidelines for managers might be established; quantitative and qualitative diversity performance measures might be developed, and diversity mission statements established (Wentling and Palma-Rivas 1997c: 23).

Most common diversity initiatives

From this survey Wentling and Palma-Rivas created a list of the diversity initiatives which were most frequently cited. All of the respondents stressed the key role of senior management in the process, whose role included such things as communicating throughout the organisation the importance of diversity as a business issue through policy statements, memos, letters, speeches, company newsletters and newspapers, and reports. (Wentling and Palma-Rivas 1997: 26). All corporations used consultants in some way to help with their diversity initiatives; some had a team of internal consultants, some used external consultants. All were trying to increase the representation of women and what is called in the US 'people of colour' at the managerial level. All had special initiatives to recruit and promote women and people of colour, and most had initiatives aimed at increasing their retention. Seven out of the eight companies had diversity awareness and diversity skills training for managers and employees, with five of them offering diversity training to senior management. Three quarters of the participants' corporations had methods for measuring the diversity performance, and over half of the companies had a diversity council to monitor how diversity issues relate to each organisational function. Over half of the corporations had initiatives dealing with management accountability related to diversity performance. Managers are held accountable for developing diversity action plans to meet their business unit and corporate goals and objectives, and diversity performance at both the business unit level and the individual level is then linked to compensation (Wentling and Palma-Rivas 1997: 31). Some examples of quantitative indicators of diversity performance were the number of women and minorities hired, the number of women and minorities promoted, the retention rates of women and minorities, and the level of employee complaints. Other measures might be employee attitude surveys of management behaviour, focus groups, employee satisfaction surveys, exit interviews, former employee surveys and self-evaluations (Wentling and Palma-Rivas 1997c: 32).

Five of the eight corporations allowed employee networks or support groups. These groups provide a forum where members can share common experiences and concerns and become resources to each other, and where career guidance information can be exchanged. Examples are groups of women, African Americans, Hispanics, or Asian Americans. They may sometimes evolve into 'advocacy groups' that negotiate with management on career development and other issues (Wentling and Palma-Rivas 1997c: 33–34). Advantages of such employee networks are that they can assist in the process of employee retention, or that they can provide feedback on diversity management performance and other company policies. (Not everyone agrees that these are unequivocally a good thing – some argue that there is a danger that they might become internally divisive and provoke a backlash from other employees, or they may take on the traits of unions and confuse existing formal procedures for handling disputes[3]).

The research participants were requested to identify the dimensions of diversity that their corporations had addressed most. Given that in theory diversity management is supposed to encompass a range of dimensions, it was noticeable that all of the corporations studied placed a very strong emphasis on 'race' and gender. One respondent stated:

> Diversity should include all differences, but the first major focus should be on race and gender. The reason for this focus is that you cannot get to more sophisticated aspects of diversity such as appreciation of diversity and diversity of thought if you cannot deal effectively with very visual diversity such as race and gender. The United Stated has not dealt effectively with race and gender, and with global competition coming we have to get serious about it now, or we are going to lose our competitive advantage (Wentling and Palma-Rivas 1997c: 39).

All of the corporations put a great emphasis on improving the representation of women and people of colour at the managerial level.

Evaluation of diversity initiatives

Six of the eight organisations reported that they evaluated their diversity initiatives, although to do this effectively was reported to be difficult and time-consuming. Six of them used surveys of employees, for example, asking for employees' perceptions one to two years after an original employee survey was conducted, to give the organisation a basis for comparison from the point at which it began the initial diversity initiative. Six stated that over time they monitored data on employees, such as labour turnover rates, retention, hiring, and promotion of women and minorities, to evaluate the effectiveness of diversity initiatives. This also showed whether people from diverse groups were represented at all levels of the organisation, especially at top management level. (Other statistics which might be used are those on absenteeism and grievance complaints.) Three of the respondents reported that their corporations used focus groups as a method for evaluating diversity initiatives. The focus groups were used to gather information from employees to determine their perception about the progress of diversity initiatives in the organisation. Another three used 'benchmarking', to assess the company's progress in relation to other companies who are seen as exemplary in addressing diversity (Wentling and Palma-Rivas 1997c: 45).

Effectiveness of diversity initiatives

The research participants were asked to identify the particular diversity initiatives that are the most effective in their corporations. Seven out of the eight indicated that

---

3   HR Magazine (Society for Human Resources Management): www.shrm.org/diversity/empnetworks1.htm.

education and training diversity initiatives were amongst the most effective. Half of them stated that performance and accountability diversity initiatives were amongst the most effective ones. Examples of these were the use of diversity accountability guidelines for managers, rewarding employee behaviour that reinforces diversity, and quantifying diversity performance measures. However, although many diversity initiatives were identified as effective, many of the respondents emphasised that no single diversity activity, used in isolation, is likely to address the problem effectively, but should instead be seen as part of an overall and comprehensive diversity strategic plan that includes many initiatives together (Wentling and Palma-Rivas 1997c: 40).

The study participants were asked to specify how effective the corporation's overall diversity initiatives had been. Six of the eight participants stated that the diversity initiatives had been very effective, with a positive impact on employees and the organisation. Two others stated that it was too early to judge the impact of the diversity initiatives. One of the respondents could point to statistical evidence on the improvement of the position of women in the organisation; others drew on more subjective indicators, such as the positive feedback they get from their employees from presentations on diversity and the diversity training efforts (Wentling and Palma-Rivas 1997c: 47). Nevertheless, some important aspects were identified as very difficult to evaluate. Six of the study participants indicated that impact of diversity on profitability was difficult to evaluate, and another six stated that impact of diversity on productivity was difficult to evaluate. The problem was that profitability and productivity are influenced by so many factors that it was difficult to isolate the specific diversity initiatives that caused the increased productivity or profit levels efforts (Wentling and Palma-Rivas 1997c: 47–48). Three respondents stated that it was difficult to evaluate the changes in employee behaviour and attitudes that were due to the diversity programme, as these changes may take a long time to occur and may go unnoticed (Wentling and Palma-Rivas 1997c: 48).

Despite the fact that the effectiveness of diversity initiatives is difficult to evaluate, the diversity management literature is characterised by case studies where companies emphasise the perceived benefits of their diversity policies. In 1994 a US federal commission on the economic imperative of managing diversity concluded 'Organizations which excel at leveraging diversity (including the hiring and advancement of women and nonwhite men into senior management jobs, and providing a climate conducive to contributions from people of diverse backgrounds) will experience better financial performance in the long run than organizations which are not effective in managing diversity.' The report cited a study that found that the stock market performance of the firms that were 'high performers' on goals relating to equal opportunities was 2½ times higher than that of firms which had invested little in such issues.[4]

---

4   M. Lauber 'Studies show that diversity in workplace is profitable' www.villagelife. org/news/archives/diversity.html.

The 'normality' of diversity management in the US

Now, at least for the bigger corporations, it seems that in the US a diversity management policy is a relatively normal and uncontroversial business practice. Among the various 'Fortune Lists' of company performance there is now one called 'Best for Minorities' which ranks companies on different quantitative and qualitative measures, such as how well minorities are represented in the general workforce, how many are among the most senior officials and highest-paid employees, whether minorities are promoted into management at the same rates as non-minority employees, and whether managers are held financially accountable for meeting diversity goals (Mor Barak 2005: 241). Of the top 50 companies on the list, Fortune magazine states 'Each of these companies takes extraordinary care to recruit and retain a diverse workforce – even, in some cases, at the cost of throwing over the old culture and constructing a new, more inclusive one in its place.'[5]

One indicator of the seriousness with which companies now take diversity policies is said to be the evidence that a commitment to diversity is being maintained even during a time of economic downturn. One major Californian computer workstation manufacturer was forced to lay off 1,000 workers, ten per cent of its workforce. One of the criteria it used in deciding the lay-offs was that of diversity, so that the company monitored its workforce to make sure that its diversity mix was maintained and that no one group of employees was disproportionately affected. One commentator made the point that traditionally a diversity programme might have been seen as a luxury, an indulgence for when times are good. 'But sticking with that commitment during a souring economy is something new, and a signal of how seriously corporate America now takes diversity'.[6]

The historical evolution of diversity management in the US

Lorbiecki and Jack (2000) suggest that a sequence of historical changes can be identified in the evolution of diversity management in the US. They set out what they describe as 'interesting twists and turns' in the evolution of diversity management, and identify 'four main turns in ideas' in its development.[7] These are demographic, political, economic and critical. Lorbiecki and Jack identify the beginning of the *demographic* phase with the publication of the report, *Workforce 2000* (Johnston and Packer 1987) which caused American business people and academics to take note of the increasingly heterogeneous workforce in the US, and the declining proportion of white males. The *political* phase began when it was realised that diversity management thinking constituted an acceptable and palatable alternative in the context of the new-Right political assault on affirmative action which began with the Reagan government. The *economic* phase came later with the publication in the early 1990s of economic arguments that organisations would suffer in terms

---

5   Fortune.com, 10 July 2000.

6   Fortune.com, 9 July 2001.

7   Lorbiecki and Jack warn that although for ease of reference they have identified these singly, in practice they are parts of interlocking, continuous strands (2000: 20).

of their performance and image if they did not pay immediate attention to managing diversity. Finally, the *critical* phase came when problems were encountered in the implementation of diversity management. From some people came a sense of frustration and disappointment that diversity initiatives had failed to deliver their promises of greater equality within the workforce as a whole. There has also developed a critical academic literature questioning some of the underlying paradigms and assumptions of diversity management (some of these are reviewed in Chapter 5).

Differences in the US and European contexts

The next question to ask is whether the trajectory of development of diversity management in the US has any parallel in the European context. The historical and political context of diversity management in Europe is different in many significant ways from that in the US. For example, there has been nothing like the US experience with affirmative action in Europe, and therefore no parallel political movement against it. It is therefore by no means clear that the classification of stages identified by Lorbiecki and Jack in the evolution of diversity management in the US has any meaning in the EU context.

Whilst the four stages suggested by Lorbiecki and Jack may not be so relevant to the European context, it may be that the pressures for the adoption of the practice, and the form and content of its development may parallel the US experience. Most of the major demographic, organisational and structural developments which have stimulated diversity management in the US can also be said to apply in Europe. Nevertheless, even though diversity management has become relatively 'unremarkable' in the US, this does not necessarily mean that the same thing will happen in Europe. There may be some factors within the US that make it a more sympathetic environment for diversity management than in the European context, or it may be that the emphasis and shape of diversity management policies in Europe will develop in different ways.

For one thing, there may be differences between the US and EU context in the factors which pressure companies to adopt diversity management policies in the first place. For example, the size of the US minority ethnic population is more than a quarter whereas in EU countries it often lies around five or six per cent. Furthermore, the US has long had relatively strong anti-discrimination legislation, contract compliance and affirmative action which have set the historical context for diversity management and its antecedents. Alongside this is a much greater readiness to resort to the courts in cases of 'race' and sex bias, and the existence of far greater financial penalties for transgressions. As mentioned earlier, in 1996 a racial discrimination lawsuit against the oil company Texaco resulted in an award of over \$176m (Wentling and Palma-Rivas 1997c: 8). In Europe there has been nothing like laws and practices of this strength, not even in the UK (Ratcliffe 2004).

Before the advent of the EU anti-discrimination directives in 2003, there had been several comparative analyses of the workings of national anti-discrimination law, and of enforcement agencies, in Europe, highlighting the wide variation in the effectiveness of such laws between EU countries (Forbes and Mead 1992; CEC 1993, MacEwen 1995; MacEwen 1997). In some European countries in the 1990s there was virtually no legal pressure on employers to avoid racial discrimination. In some cases, legislation against employment discrimination did not cover the private sector. Even when strong law existed in theory, there were problems in practice. The case of France is an example where problems were experienced with the use of the criminal law against racism and discrimination, and cases of employment discrimination seldom brought to court for lack of concrete evidence (De Rudder et al. 1995). In Sweden, during the year following the introduction of the 1994 law against employment discrimination, not one case of alleged discrimination found its way to a work tribunal, even though the Discrimination Ombudsman had received 75 complaints from members of the public (Graham and Soininen 1998).

Clearly, then, there has been relatively little legal pressure on European employers to introduce such policies when compared with the situation in the US. Of course, this has started to change with the coming into force of the two new EU anti-discrimination directives – Council Directive 2000/43/EC (the Racial Equality Directive) and Council Directive 2000/78/EC (the Employment Equality Directive). All of the 'old' 15 member states were obliged to complete transposition by July 2003 (in the case of Directive 2000/43/EC) and by 2 December 2003 for most of the provisions in Directive 2000/78/EC. The 10 'new' member states were obliged to transpose the directives by May 2004. The implications of the anti-discrimination directives for stimulating diversity management in the EU are potentially very significant. As Mor Barak (2005: 212) observes: 'Equal rights legislation and affirmative positive action policies are prerequisites for the development of diversity management because they create the social, legal, and organizational environment on which diversity management initiatives can be based'. (The implications of the directives will be considered further in Chapter 4.)

Another thing to remember is that the US companies on the Fortune lists described earlier, and those in the Wentling and Palma-Rivas survey, were all large corporations, many of them multinational enterprises. It is argued that diversity policies are more likely to find sympathetic homes in larger companies. Whilst more than 75 per cent of the Fortune 1000 companies in the US in 2001 had some sort of diversity initiative,[8] other companies were less likely to have them. For example, a survey carried out in 1998 found out that whilst three quarters of Fortune 500 companies had diversity programmes that had been developed more than five years previously, only 36 per cent of companies in general had a diversity programme.[9] This factor could be relevant for our European focus, as in some European countries a much higher proportion of business activity takes place in small and medium-sized companies than in others. Denmark, for example, is a country characterised by relatively small businesses, many of them without anything like a formal human resources function. As Glastra et al. (1998: 172) state in connection with the Netherlands:

---

8   Fortune.com, 9 July 2001.

9   Society for Human Resource Management press release, www.shrm.org.

Equity policies have far less salience in smaller firms (…) Such firms often lack the human resources capacity to address legal requirements (…) while they may feel much more dependent on a stable workforce. Hence it might not be very realistic to expect them to follow the example set by larger corporations…

These kinds of differences between the US and EU provide the starting point for the next two chapters. Chapter 3 looks at the background context for the development of diversity management in Europe and Chapter 4 looks at some of the implications for diversity management of differences which exist between the US and Europe, as well as of the differences which exist between EU countries themselves.

Chapter 3

The Background to Diversity Management in Europe

Whilst it may be possible to trace the origins and lineage of diversity management in the US through certain historical stages, the developmental stages of diversity management in Europe seem to be less clearly defined. Of course, many of the structural factors said to have lain behind the development of diversity management in the US – demographic changes, globalisation, the growth in diverse markets, the expansion of the service sector, organisational developments – also apply in the European context, and create similar pressures on European enterprises. What is more, the Europeans have had the example of the earlier US and Canadian experience to learn from. American-owned companies in the EU became exposed to diversity management ideas from the parent company, and some European managers and consultants came back from visits to America and Canada enthused with the new idea to spread the word back home. However, as well as these, diversity management in Europe also had some home grown roots, and some of these were qualitatively different to the US.

Intercultural management

One of the roots of diversity management in Europe lay in established practices of intercultural management in regard to companies which operate internationally. The theory and practice of intercultural management arose in opposition to the earlier prevailing assumption that there is 'one best way' in management practice, and that the values of the parent company can be simply maintained in foreign subsidiaries. By this earlier assumption, cultural diversity had been threatening. The alternative is the 'polycentric approach':

> The polycentric approach begins with the idea that a universal strategy is not possible and that international businesses should accommodate to the local situation: 'When in Rome, do as the Romans do' … Diversity is allowed and appreciated and monitoring from above is substituted by relative autonomy of local branches (Koot 1997: 325).

The academic discipline of intercultural management became relatively well established in some European universities. When, in European countries of immigration, an awareness began to develop that the post–World War II labour migrants were not in fact 'guestworkers' but were developing into settled ethnic minority communities which would continue to maintain some aspects of cultural identity and practice, then intercultural management practices became seen to be relevant to home-based enterprises and not only to companies with overseas branches.

The origins of diversity management in the two regions of North America and Europe reflect two different strands which co-exist within the practice: the desire to produce a fair and equitable work environment by combating discrimination and furthering equal opportunities, and the recognition of the need to enhance integration by making practical allowances for cultural difference. In the US it was the former which was dominant, operating through the equal employment opportunity legislation, whereas in Europe the role of the second one as the initial stimulus to action seemed to be stronger. This difference corresponds to different paradigms between North America and Europe regarding immigration and ethnic diversity – the former reflects the region's 'historical role in absorbing immigrants' and 'a value system rooted in equal employment opportunity, antidiscrimination and fairness paradigms' (Mor Barak 2005: 155) whereas the latter reflects Europe's dominant focus on the 'problems' of migrant workers and strategies to 'integrate' immigrants into the existing labour market and employment structures of individual countries.

Equal opportunities and anti-discrimination policies

Whilst the legal and administrative pressure on companies through equal employment opportunities/affirmative action (EEO/AA) were peculiar to the US, there are some countries in Europe, notably the Netherlands and the UK, where legislation also provided a stimulus to practices of equal opportunity policies in organisations. There also developed within these countries a body of expertise, a tradition of consultants and a class of experts within management similar to the human resource professionals in the US, described by Kelly and Dobbin (1998), who developed into the American diversity advocates and specialists of later times (see Chapter 5). As well as this, there were some campaigns about how good business practice is reflected in the employment of a diverse workforce, even if these were not yet voiced in the specific language of diversity management. Having said this, the difference of the EU context is that these were not widespread, and, as indicated in the preceding chapter, in most member states there was nothing like the legal pressure for action found in the US. Within Europe, the great variety in legal and institutional context between countries led to enormous differences in anti-discrimination cases regarding employment. For example, Professor Michael Banton, past chair of the UN Committee for the Elimination of Racial Discrimination, pointed out in 2000 during a lecture in Stockholm[1] that for the year 1997 he could find no cases of racial discrimination in employment being put forward for legal consideration in Sweden; in France during that year there were four cases, and in the UK there were 3,173 cases.[2] Clearly these immense national differences were more a reflection of the

---

1   'An international perspective on the Swedish prohibition of ethnic discrimination' Conference: *Ras och Diskriminering,* Ombudsmannen mot Etnisk Diskriminering, Stockholm December 2000.

2   These were cases lodged with ACAS, the UK's Advisory, Conciliation and Arbitration Service. http://www.acas.org.uk.

degree of 'user-friendliness' of each country's legal system for complaining, rather than of the reality of employment discrimination itself. Banton calculated that if the levels of ethnic discrimination in the workplace were similar, and if the ratio of cases to total population were held constant, then the Swedish figure should have been 509 cases. (Note that this was before the subsequent improvement in Swedish anti-discrimination legislation.)

EU influence on anti-discrimination practice

In the context of the wide variety in levels of awareness and practices within the EU, there was a growing influence of EU-wide institutions which were attempting to raise awareness and change practices regarding racial and ethnic discrimination in employment. In the UK, which had more closely followed the American tradition, there was a reasonably developed awareness of employment discrimination, as reflected in legislation, in organisational practices and in academic traditions. However, it is probably true to say that in Europe as a whole the pressure on policy from a knowledge of discrimination and a desire to do something about it was much less a stimulus to action than had been the case in the US. This began to change in Europe during the 1990s, with the increasing evidence of research, the lobbying of NGOs and immigrant organisations, and awareness-raising initiatives such as the 'European Year Against Racism' in 1997. The wide variation in experience between countries within the EU gave added significance to the factor of the pressure from the European Commission on combating discrimination and disseminating good practice on the employment integration of Europe's immigrants and ethnic minorities.

Within the EU, guidelines by European institutions are increasingly important in influencing labour market interventions at a national level, and behind some of these exhortations are European directives on the subject which have legal force. A directive is an instrument which lays down a common basis in goals to be achieved through legislation, whilst allowing each national government the flexibility to achieve this according to the different legal systems and conditions in their respective national contexts. As described earlier, the Racial Equality Directive to implement equal treatment irrespective of racial or ethnic origin was adopted in 2000, and prohibits discrimination in relation to access to employment and training, and to working conditions. This means that employers within each country need to ensure that principles of equal treatment on questions of racial and ethnic origin apply to their actions regarding their own workforces. Article 13 of the Racial Equality Directive also states that member states must designate 'a body or bodies for the promotion of equal treatment of all persons without discrimination on the grounds of racial or ethnic origin'. The competences of such bodies should include providing independent assistance to victims of discrimination in pursuing their complaints about discrimination, conducting independent surveys concerning discrimination, and publishing independent reports and making recommendations on issues relating to discrimination (EUMC 2006a).

However, even before this directive was passed, EU institutions were pressing the 'social partners' – the trade union and employers organisations – for action, and were stimulating the exchange of examples of voluntary good practice between member states. Behind this was the growing research evidence on racial discrimination in European labour markets and workplaces, countering the 'no problem here' assumption which had been widespread until the 1990s. In particular there was evidence on racial discrimination from comparative research sponsored by international bodies that were able to use their influence and position to disseminate the findings to political, business and trade union leaders.

One of these research reports was that commissioned by the European Foundation for the Improvement of Living and Working Conditions, Dublin, covering all of the (then) 15 EU countries plus Norway. This used national researchers in all 16 countries to bring together evidence of widespread 'racial' or ethnic discrimination in its direct forms, such as the refusal to employ people simply on the grounds of colour of skin or ethnic background, as well as indirect discrimination, such as restricting employment opportunities to the family of existing workers, or using questionable informal and subjective criteria in recruitment. The report also illustrated a general ignorance of the problems of racism and discrimination in employment on the part of many European employers, trade unionists, labour inspectors, and so on (Wrench 1996).

A second source of evidence in the 1990s was the ILO initiative 'Combating discrimination against (im)migrant workers and ethnic minorities in the world of work'. The first part of this consisted of a testing programme using matched pairs of testers making applications for the same jobs. The applicants would be identical in all job-relevant respects; one would be from a white majority background, the other of ethnic minority origin. On average, in roughly one third of cases where offers were made, the minority candidate was excluded from the offer. Frequently the minority applicant would be told the job had gone, whilst an enquiry a little later by the majority applicant would discover that the vacancy was still in fact available. This demonstrated that racial discrimination in access to employment was of significant importance in the four European countries[3] where the ILO research was initially carried out: the Netherlands, Germany, Spain and Belgium (Bovenkerk et al. 1995, Goldberg et al. 1995, Colectivo Ioé 1996, Arrijn et al. 1998). At the same time, an independent project based on the ILO's methodology was carried out in Denmark, with similar results (Hjarnø and Jensen 1997).[4] (An overview of the results of the first four countries in the ILO's discrimination testing programme can be found in Zegers de Beijl 2000.)

Therefore, by the time of the European Year Against Racism in 1997, the issue of employment discrimination – and, correspondingly, the issue of anti-discrimination measures to combat this – was firmly on the EU agenda.

---

3   In the UK, the evidence of discrimination had already been provided by this method outside the ILO project – e.g. Hubbuck and Carter 1980, Esmail and Everington 1993, Simpson and Stevenson 1994. In 2004 the ILO published the results of testing carried out in a fifth country, Italy – see Allasino et al. 2004.

4   Later another study replicated the methodology in Switzerland: Fibbi et al. 2003.

European pressure for voluntary measures

There were several initiatives in the 1990s which deserve particular attention as measures or campaigns to promote the greater dissemination and adoption of organisational good practice in this field. One of these was the *Joint Declaration on the Prevention of Racial Discrimination and Xenophobia and Promotion of Equal Treatment at the Workplace*, signed by the social partner organisations in Florence in October 1995. The second is the earlier-mentioned ILO programme *Combating discrimination against (im)migrant workers and ethnic minorities in the world of work*. The third is the *European Compendium of Good Practice for the Prevention of Racism at the Workplace*, an EC report launched in Lisbon at the end of the 1997 European Year Against Racism. The fourth is the report *Gaining from Diversity*, an initiative of the European Business Network for Social Cohesion with the support of the European Commission, also as part of the European Year Against Racism. Thus three out of the four are to some degree initiatives of the European Commission.

The next section will consider in turn each of these four. The exercise will serve more than one function. Firstly it will provide information relevant to the development of diversity management in Europe over the 1990s. Secondly, it will illustrate the value of typologies to classify and evaluate organisational practices in an international context, and will provide empirical material to form the basis of a new classificatory typology of organisational initiatives against racial and ethnic discrimination. The aim of this typology is to enable us to put into context and better comprehend developments under the heading of diversity management, and related initiatives, in EU member states.

The 1995 Joint Declaration

The European Social Partners signed the Joint Declaration on the Prevention of Racial Discrimination and Xenophobia and Promotion of Equal Treatment at the Workplace in Florence in October 1995. The aim was to foster good practice in these areas on the grounds that 'Legal protection is not itself sufficient to eliminate racist and xenophobic behaviour and feelings'.

The preamble to the Joint Declaration opens with a strong moral statement against racism, affirming the importance that the social partners attach to the achievement in Europe of 'a democratic, pluralistic society characterised by solidarity and respect for the dignity of all human beings'. It continues 'Elimination of all forms of racial discrimination and promotion of equal opportunity are fundamental values of the common cultural heritage and legal traditions of all European states.' Having said this, from then on the main justifications for the actions recommended in the Joint Declaration are in fact economic. 'Racism and xenophobia constitute a serious threat, not only to the stability of European society, but also to the smooth functioning of the economy.' The Declaration then draws on the kinds of arguments which have been used to justify diversity management practice in America. For example, the declaration states:

Organisations are operating in an increasingly multicultural environment with customers, suppliers and employees from diverse national, ethnic and cultural back-grounds. Success in the marketplace is more and more dependent on the ability to maximise the potential of these diverse backgrounds. Organisations which achieve this will be more competitive and better able to cope successfully with change.

Yet, it argues, despite this, 'European economies are not using the value which their diverse workforces can offer to their full potential.' Some of the arguments to encourage action against racism, xenophobia and discrimination mirror exactly those in the diversity management literature, for example:

- 'Using people's talents to the full' ... 'An organisation made up of diverse groups, with a wide range of abilities, experience and skills, is more likely to be alive to new ideas and different possibilities ...'
- 'Making the company more attractive to customers and clients' ... At a time of labour and skill, shortages 'young people will be more likely to want to join employers with a good track record of providing equal opportunity' and 'customers and clients are increasingly likely to prefer dealing with a company which ensures that its suppliers and contractors have fair employment practices'.
- 'Getting closer to customers and understanding their needs' .... Given the growth of ethnic minority and international markets, a diverse workforce is a potential source of accurate and unbiased information about existing and potential customers.
- 'Operating internationally with success' ... 'Organisations which attract a diverse workforce and are alert to their skills, talents, experience and contacts are in a good position to reach and attract new markets in those countries where their employees have connections.'
- 'Avoiding the costs of discrimination' ... Racial discrimination result in legal penalties, as well as adverse publicity, damage to staff development, higher absenteeism, and greater staff turnover.

The Joint Declaration then recommends a range of measures that can make a positive contribution towards preventing discrimination at the workplace. The kinds of things included here are standard components of an organisational equal opportunities policy. These include widening the sources of recruitment by advertising in publications read by ethnic minorities and using employment services and agencies in multiethnic areas, ensuring that job descriptions do not contain arbitrary and unnecessary criteria, avoiding demands for unnecessarily high levels of language mastery, ensuring that interviewers are aware of issues of discrimination and are trained to avoid unjustified and irrelevant selection criteria, offering pre-work training courses or work experience to members of minority groups, and having clear procedures for dealing with discrimination, including disciplinary procedures.

These are largely those measures which are categorised later in this chapter as 'organisational equal opportunity policies with elements of positive action.' Although the word 'diverse' appears a few times, there is no mention at all of 'diversity management' in the Joint Declaration. As we have seen earlier, a defining feature of diversity management is the recognition and practical allowance of cultural differences. In the Joint Declaration there is only one, very weak, exhortation to the kind of action in respect of cultural diversity which is so prominent in a diversity management approach. Under the heading of 'Respect for cultural and religious differences' the last recommendation in the Joint Declaration states 'In order to meet the needs of a heterogeneous workforce, it may be useful to explore and take into account the specific cultural or religious needs of certain groups, insofar as they may be accommodated in the organisation'. This is a rather tentative statement, and probably reflects the fact that in Europe in 1995 there was still relatively little consciousness of diversity management and its associated cultural emphasis as an anti-discrimination practice.

The ILO anti-discrimination training project

This second initiative employed a categorisation of anti-discrimination activity in Europe which did include the category of diversity management. Whilst it showed that diversity management was still very much a minority activity, it also produced indications of its growing development.

The previously mentioned ILO research programme had drawn attention to discrimination through the testing experiments. A later stage of the same programme looked at one measure to combat this, namely the extent, content and impact of anti-discrimination training and education activities in migrant-receiving countries. This was carried out in the Netherlands, the UK, Finland, Spain and Belgium (see Abell et al. 1997, Taylor et al. 1997, Vuori 1997, Colectivo Ioé 1997, Castelain-Kinet et al. 1998.). The aim was to document and evaluate in different countries the effectiveness of anti-discrimination training and education activities where such training is imparted to people who have a role to play in access to the labour market, such as personnel and line managers in both the private and public sectors who are involved in the recruitment process, as well as civil servants and officials in labour exchanges and other agencies which play a placement role for individuals seeking employment, and trade union full-time officials and shop stewards.

There exist many different types of anti-discrimination training – often working from very different assumptions about the causes of and remedies for racism and discrimination. They are all directed towards gatekeepers in the labour market, and all would claim to be tackling employment discrimination. The aim of this part of the ILO's initiative was to classify and document the different anti-discrimination training activities in various countries, and also, if possible, come to some conclusions about whether certain training approaches seem to be more useful than others, and in what circumstances. By 'approaches' is meant the underlying philosophies and assumptions of such training, and the corresponding methodologies and training content implied by these.

As part of the project, a new typology was created which enabled researchers to classify the anti-discrimination training activities in different countries. The typology was modified from an earlier one on combating racism through training for service delivery staff (Luthra and Oakley 1991). The basis of the typology was certain regularities of strategy and content which have run through much equal opportunities/anti-discrimination training, culminating in the latest type, that of training as part of a diversity management policy. The main training approaches were categorised as follows (Wrench and Taylor 1993: 16).

(1) Information Training
(2) Cultural Awareness Training
(3) Racism Awareness Training
(4) Equalities Training
(5) Anti-Racism Training
(6) Diversity Training

(1) *Information Training*   This basic and rather common form of training provides demographic facts and figures on migrants, their countries of origin, their current employment patterns and so on, generally through straightforward lectures, videos or the provision of written material. It includes programmes to encourage inter-cultural awareness and promote better communication and understanding. The assumption behind this approach is that most people are fair, but are often unaware of the extent and effect of racial discrimination. Training is required to inform them about discrimination and disadvantage in society, so that they will be disposed to implement measures to tackle it. A corresponding assumption is that the provision of correct information is enough to lead to behavioural change.

(2) *Cultural Awareness Training*   This not only provides cultural information, but actively engages trainees in exercises to change their attitudes; for example, role play exercises, or intensive group discussions. Courses of cultural awareness might include material on the majority culture of the trainees on the grounds that thinking critically about their own culture will help in understanding others better. Courses on the theme of 'living/working together with foreigners/migrants' will often fall under this heading. Although Cultural Awareness Training, unlike simple Information Training, is more active in trying to produce attitude change in the trainees, it still remains similar to Information Training in seeing behavioural change as relatively unproblematic. Implicit in this approach is the idea that raising trainees' awareness and changing prejudiced attitudes will thereby automatically reduce discriminatory behaviour.

(3) *Racism Awareness Training*   This approach is typified by the 'Human Awareness' or 'White Awareness' programme of Katz (1978) in the USA and those who follow her model. The premise of Racism Awareness Training is that racism is located in white people and operates to their interests; it is therefore their responsibility to tackle it. The methods are generally techniques to induce self-awareness in a group setting, with trainers sometimes using confrontational techniques, along with role-play and other self-awareness exercises. The narrow focus of this training is on racism itself, with the aim of producing a relatively rapid change in attitudes, and an assumption that this will produce change at the behavioural level.

(4) *Equalities Training* (This type might also be known as 'Equal Opportunities Training'.) In complete contrast to Racism Awareness Training which seeks to change attitudes, Equalities Training refers to training which is designed primarily to affect behaviour. The training seeks to side-step attitudes by seeing them as private and irrelevant to the job, and simply aims to instruct the trainees in legally or professionally appropriate behaviour. This is defined as precisely as possible in terms of the appropriate norms and behaviour, and the required skills. In many countries the starting point of Equalities Training will be that the law proscribes racial discrimination and that agencies and professionals must therefore make sure that discrimination, whether deliberate or unintentional, does not occur.

(5) *Anti-Racism Training* Anti-Racism Training was developed after disillusion with Racism Awareness Training, retaining a strong commitment to combating racism directly, whilst seeking to change organisational practice rather than individual self-awareness. The premise of this approach is that racism cannot be simply reduced to a problem of (white) individuals, and yet neither can it be tackled purely in terms of discriminatory behaviour without addressing the level of personal attitudes and awareness. The goal is to secure the support of individuals in challenging the racism which is endemic in the culture and institutions of the society, and Anti-Racism Training forms part of an organisational strategy designed to pursue this aim. Although this approach would seek to tackle racial discrimination in recruitment, the approach seeks to combat racism at all levels in the organisation, not simply at this point of entry.

(6) *Diversity Training* This is the most recent development, stimulated by diversity management programmes in the United States (Thomas 1990, Jamieson and O'Mara 1991, Kossek and Lobel 1996). As shown in Chapter 1, diversity management is seen as the logical next step after measures such as equal opportunities initiatives and affirmative action programmes have broken down barriers to the employment of minorities, producing a more diverse workforce. The training, which is mainly directed at managers, emphasises the importance of valuing difference. It argues that ethnic, racial and sexual groups have different cultural styles of working which should not be negatively labelled by white managers. The objective is not to assimilate minorities (and women) into the dominant white (and male) organisational culture but to create a dominant heterogeneous culture. Being the latest and broadest type, it is likely to include elements of many of the other types: for example, awareness exercises on 'racial sensibility' similar to Racism Awareness Training; sessions on cultural sensitivity as found in Cultural Awareness Training; or strategies of fair recruitment, as found in Equalities Training. It might aim to produce individual attitude and behaviour change as well as long-term organisational change.

Application of the typology in Europe

This six-fold typology was incorporated into a standardised research manual (Wrench and Taylor 1993) which provided a common methodological framework for comparing case studies of training practice in different countries. From this exercise we can get an illustration of some countries where a diversity management approach was starting to become more common, and an indication in others of what might be called 'pre-diversity management' conditions. This can be seen in the application of the typology in five of the ILO's national studies: those of the UK, the Netherlands, Spain, Finland and Belgium (Wrench 2001).

The UK context

The UK report documented the activities of a sample of 57 training providers, most being independent training consultants. Training in the UK was found to have progressed beyond the simple information provision of the Information Training type, although the provision of factual information on problems of racism and discrimination, and the legal context, was still part of the syllabus of other types of training. Nor was there any evidence that the formerly common types of 'attitude change' training, Cultural Awareness Training and Racism Awareness Training, were used any more. Most of the current training activity could be classified as 'Equalities Training', the defining characteristic of which is to provide skills and change behaviour. By far the most common activity here was the imparting of skills for fairness in recruitment and selection. There was also some Anti-Racism Training. However, a relatively new development was the increasing use of Diversity Training, the approach which emphasises the benefits of a diverse workforce, linking, for example, productivity gains to identifying, valuing and drawing upon cultural differences within a workforce. This trend was noticeable, even after having made allowances for the fact that some trainers mis-labelled their courses as 'diversity training' simply to take advantage of the current fashion (Taylor et al. 1997: 60).

In the UK study, as with other national reports, case studies of different training types were selected, and these were used to discover the reactions of trainers, clients, and trainees to the training experience. In terms of the reactions of the participants, the most common type of training – Equalities Training – came out best in this study, and many participants were able to relate how changes in behaviour and in working practices were positively achieved. However, the responses to Diversity Training were quite mixed. The relatively pure and narrow form of 'valuing diversity' approach aroused little positive reaction. Often trainees felt that diversity management was something which needed to follow on from, rather than replace, effective anti-discrimination and equal opportunities policies. Indeed, in its original formulation, diversity management works on the assumption that barriers to the employment of minorities have already largely been broken down, resulting in a diverse workforce. Trainees felt that as this stage had not been reached, Diversity Training was a little premature. However, in those cases where Diversity Training included the anti-discrimination elements of Anti-Racism Training and Equalities Training, then trainees were far more positive about its impact (Taylor et al. 1997).

The Netherlands context

The Dutch researchers (Abell et al. 1997) found that most of the activities of the Dutch 'inter-cultural management' training providers were classifiable as Information Training and Cultural Awareness Training, although it seems that Information Training was no longer given alone, but rather in combination with some form of Cultural Awareness Training. Of a sample of 54 training providers, almost half the courses fell into the category of Cultural Awareness Training. In contrast to the UK, Equalities Training in its narrower type – primarily instructing trainees in legally and professionally appropriate behaviour to avoid discrimination in recruitment and selection – seemed to be provided only rarely in the Netherlands. Racism Awareness Training was also not common in the Netherlands, and, unlike the UK, had not been common in the past. Anti-Racism Training was not as popular in the Netherlands as in the UK. According to the Dutch researchers, one reason for these differences was that public discussion on issues of racism and discrimination had been more recent in the Netherlands than in the UK, and the existence of these phenomena had continued to be denied for a long time. However, in common with the UK study, the report detected a shift in training activities towards Diversity Training, mainly directed at managers, and emphasising the value of difference and the creation of a heterogeneous culture. The Dutch researchers suggest that the beginnings of a shift away from Cultural Awareness Training to Diversity Training could be seen as a step in the right direction, away from the simple 'attitude change' paradigm towards one which envisages more practical changes. Indeed, for participants in the Dutch training, their experiences of Diversity Training generally provoked more positive reactions than Cultural Awareness Training, possibly, according to Abell and his colleagues, because of the preference of trainees for more practical 'handles' (Abell et al. 1997).

The Spanish context

In the Spanish case, not only was there no evidence of diversity management, there was little evidence of the other categories of activity either. Preliminary investigation suggested the non-existence, or at best, the scant implementation of anti-discrimination programmes designed for 'gatekeepers' (Colectivo Ioé 1997). The report concluded that within the Spanish world of work there was no general awareness of a potential problem of ethnic or racial discrimination existing in the system. Indeed, an earlier stage of the ILO programme had shown that at that time Spain was one of the few industrialised migrant receiving countries which still had not introduced anti-discrimination legislation to protect non-national workers. The Spanish researchers were told that immigrants were concentrated in certain segments of the labour market, without being in competition for jobs with the majority population, and this was one reason why there was little recognition of a 'problem'. However, the research report did find evidence of the beginnings of change, with labour market actors becoming increasingly receptive to the idea of anti-discrimination training. The initiatives were coming first from people in local government, trade unions, and NGOs, with an added impetus coming from the internationalisation of enterprises which brought in experience from other countries, together with the increasing openness of Spanish officials to initiatives from the EU.[5]

The Finnish context

The Finnish report (Vuori 1997) concluded from both the literature and from the interviews carried out with 28 representatives of different sections of the labour market, that there was little evidence of anti-discrimination training in Finland at that time. Many respondents felt that racial or ethnic discrimination itself was rare, meaning that such training was unnecessary, and most people felt that there was no real demand for anti-discrimination training among labour market actors. The author of the report saw the lack of demand for anti-discrimination training as related to the lack of awareness of existing discrimination. In particular, it seemed, there was no recognition of indirect discrimination, such as the use of recruitment channels to which migrants do not have access, or unnecessary language criteria for jobs. When respondents were asked as to what training might be necessary in the future, most identified the sort which would be categorised as Information Training and Cultural Awareness Training. There was already some training of this sort targeted at civil servants working in labour exchanges to provide cultural information on migrant and ethnic minority communities, and to improve intercultural skills. A general assumption was that the provision of accurate information on ethnic minorities, and a greater cultural sensitivity in dealing with them, would be enough to prevent discrimination and ensure equal treatment for them. A conclusion drawn from the report was that 'a fundamental prerequisite for further training to be developed is a raising of the awareness of the occurrence of discrimination against migrant and ethnic minority workers – an awareness which is still lacking among many of the labour market gatekeepers interviewed for this research'.[6]

The Belgian context

One of the most notable things about the Belgian research was the researchers' discovery that in places at that time there was such an unsympathetic climate to the very notion of anti-discrimination training that it was concluded that it was probably best that any such training should be 'disguised' by integrating it into other more general training 'in order to avoid unfavourable reactions or even powerful opposition.'[7] The national report described how in Belgium, attempts to move the emphasis of anti-discrimination training away from training directed at migrants to training aimed at representatives of the societal majority met with significant

---

5   Report of regional seminar in Catalonia on the findings of the ILO programme in Spain, May 1997.

6   Foreword to the report by M.I.Abella, Vuori 1997 p.vi.

7   Report on the seminar organised in Belgium to evaluate the results of research conducted in association with the ILO project; ILO Geneva 1998.

resistance, countering some of the potential effects of anti-discrimination training measures and leading to some initiatives being discontinued (Castelain-Kinet et al. 1998).

National differences

The evidence above applies to only five EU countries in the 1990s. However, even with this limited exercise it is possible to identify factors of difference which are likely to have had implications for the later development of diversity management in different national contexts. From looking at the experiences within just these five European countries it is possible to perceive great variety in local experiences of anti-discrimination activities around the late 1990s. The Spanish example showed that at that time there was little experience or awareness of anti-discrimination training, equal opportunity policies or diversity management, because the local circumstances were so different to countries where such phenomena were more noticeably established. The Finnish report showed that there could be a lack of awareness of employment discrimination issues by key labour market actors at the same time that evidence from elsewhere was showing that organisational responses to discrimination were starting to become necessary (see Valtonen 2001), and the Belgian report showed that the very suggestion that anti-discrimination training was required could be controversial. The comparison between the UK and the Netherlands suggested that even in the case of the two EU countries with the most experience of organisational anti-discrimination policies there were differences which could have implications for the character of the subsequent development of diversity management itself within those countries.

The ILO study of anti-discrimination training was also carried out in the US, (Bendick et al. 1998) and the American study confirmed, not surprisingly, that diversity management was much more common in the US than in Europe. The American researchers compared the distribution of training emphases within the sample of training providers contacted in the US research with the equivalents indicated in the UK and the Netherlands reports. It is interesting to note that in each of these three countries in the mid-1990s the training emphasis was different. In the Netherlands, the most common activity was Cultural Awareness Training, with nearly half the trainers involved in this. In the UK the majority activity was Equalities Training, with nearly 60 per cent involvement. In the US, although the largest category was still Equalities Training, Diversity Training was now almost as large, involving over a third of trainers (Bendick et al. 1998: 34).

Drawing on the evidence of the ILO study, we can raise a question in the context of the spread of diversity management in Europe. Between different parts of Europe in the 1990s there was clearly great variation in the levels of awareness of racial discrimination in employment, in the definition of it as a problem issue, and in the experience in organisational policies to combat it. Did this have implications for the character of any diversity management practices which might develop in these different contexts? For example, would the historically strong Dutch tradition of intercultural management, as reflected in the dominance of Cultural Awareness

Training, mean that diversity management in the Netherlands might be stronger on cultural elements and weaker on the combating discrimination elements, compared to the UK, where the dominance of Equalities training to combat discriminatory behaviour might mean that anti-discrimination elements figure more strongly? Since the Finnish ILO study was completed, the ideas of diversity management have been discussed and put on the agenda in Finland, starting with a conference on the subject which took place in Helsinki in September 2000.[8] Will the development of diversity management in Finland take on a different form to that in the US or even in the UK simply because of the apparent absence of experience of previous organisational approaches in Finland?

The typology used in the ILO study demonstrated the value of such devices in international comparisons. However, the focus on anti-discrimination training was too narrow for this typology to be of real value in monitoring the development of diversity management in Europe, as anti-discrimination training is only one potential component of a diversity management approach. A new broader typology of organisational practices is therefore needed, and part of the material to construct this comes from the next two European initiatives in the 1990s.

European Compendium of Good Practice

The third initiative was the European Compendium of Good Practice for the Prevention of Racism at the Workplace. The final section of the 1995 Joint Declaration on the Prevention of Racial Discrimination and Xenophobia and Promotion of Equal Treatment at the Workplace had called for a set of follow-up measures, among them the compilation of a compendium of good practice, and asked the European Foundation in Dublin to take care of its production. The Compendium of Good Practice was published in 1997, and consists of 25 case studies from the then 15 countries of the European Union. The case studies encompass private and public sector companies, trade unions, collective agreements, codes of conduct and national initiatives (Wrench 1997a).

The objectives of the Compendium were set out in the Joint Declaration on the Prevention of Racial Discrimination and Xenophobia and Promotion of Equal Treatment at the Workplace. These included identifying examples of good practice in the different member states, disseminating the information gathered so as to contribute to a broader exchange of experiences, providing guidance regarding the promotion of equal treatment and combating of racial discrimination at the workplace, and promoting the notion that it is in the interests of business to implement equal opportunities policies.

National researchers within each EU member state produced a report covering case studies of good practice within their own country, most of them concerning policies which operate at the level of an individual company or organisation. From

---

8   'Managing Diversity for Improving Business Performance in Nordic Countries' and 'Tools for Diversity Management' organised by UnICom the University of Jyväskylä, European Business Network for Social Cohesion, Ministry of Labour, Centre for Business and Diversity and Finnish Business and Society.

these, 25 case studies were selected to comprise the Compendium. Before discussing the implications of the content of these cases for our understanding of diversity management in Europe, we will look at the fourth initiative, and address these two together.

Gaining from Diversity

The fourth initiative was the report 'Gaining from Diversity' (Stewart and Lindburgh 1997). This was initiated by the European Business Network for Social Cohesion, an organisation supported by business organisations and companies across Europe whose task is to promote 'business–driven approaches to tackling social exclusion'. The report was published to coincide with the European Year Against Racism and formed part of a drive to promote the exchange of experience across Europe on the practical experiences of business in addressing the opportunities and challenges presented by Europe's ethnic diversity.

The report clearly uses the language of diversity much more than the other three initiatives. It contrasts two main organisational approaches to the inclusion of immigrant or ethnic minority workers. The first is the 'Fitting new groups into an unchanged workplace' approach, which places greatest emphasis on the 'adaptation' or 'integration' of new groups into the workplace. In businesses adopting this approach, existing procedures and practices would continue largely unchanged and there would be little expectation that the organisation would need to change to accommodate the immigrant or minority workers. The effect of this approach is that only those minority group members who fully adopt the style and approach of the majority cultures are likely to be accepted into the organisation or be able to progress within it (Stewart and Lindburgh 1997: 14).

This approach is described as a 'colour-blind' approach – all people are treated the same and colour or ethnic differences are meant to be ignored. The authors argue that the disadvantages of this approach include the operation of 'glass ceilings' or other invisible barriers which can block the progress of members of social or cultural minorities and leaves them in low grade or low status jobs. There may be a loss to the organisation of the talent and skills of the full range of potential employees from migrant or ethnic minority communities; as well as a loss of the potential for creative ideas and problem-solving from the varied perspectives of people of different backgrounds (Stewart and Lindburgh 1997: 14).

The alternative approach is 'Recognizing and valuing diversity'. This emphasises the fact that diversity or multiculturalism inherently add value to the workforce. Here, the primary aim is to achieve equality of opportunity for men and women of different backgrounds, but it is also recognised that this social and cultural diversity may mean that 'systems and procedures that are appropriate for some groups of people may be inappropriate or actually discriminatory if applied to other groups of people.' Therefore, employers who adopt this approach generally start by evaluating their personnel policies and procedures as well as the informal organisational culture 'to identify actual or potential sources of adverse impact against different groups of staff.'

The report sets out examples of business strategies under the two main headings of internal and external strategies. The latter concern initiatives such as assisting community programmes in disadvantaged areas, or giving support to ethnic minority businesses. In this analysis we will concern ourselves more with the internal strategies, which the report sees as able to assist companies in gaining from diversity. These internal strategies are categorised in three main ways:

- increasing access – promoting ethnic and cultural diversity through the recruitment process
- mobility – preparing migrants and ethnic minorities for advancement within the firm (the internal professional development of employees)
- preparing the firm for a more diverse workforce – the implications of a diverse workforce for managerial and non-managerial staff

The text of this is interspersed with examples and cases from companies and business organisations across Europe. Rather than look at these under the report's own headings, they will be considered under the headings of a new six-fold typology which can then be used to analyse the previous initiative and this one together.

A typology of organisational practices

Like the ILO anti-discrimination training study, the two reports, *Gaining from Diversity* and the *Compendium of Good Practice*, produced a wide range of examples of organisational practices across Europe. The ILO research had demonstrated the value of a typology of anti-discrimination training which facilitated the development of generalisations about practices in different countries. Typologies are important tools of analysis which allow the identification of a number of main tendencies, each with its own internal consistency, providing an agreed point of reference for defining and comparing particular forms of organisational activities (Luthra and Oakley 1991: 32). However, the ILO typology is too narrow in scope to be of use in understanding broader organisational practices such as diversity management, because anti-discrimination training is only one (potential) element of diversity management practice. Therefore, if any meaningful generalisations are to be made about organisational anti-discrimination activities in Europe, it is necessary first to organise and categorise them using a new typology. The new typology would be different to that in the ILO exercise as it has to encompass a wide variety of activities, not just training, but it should be compatible with the earlier one.

Therefore, in order to help us understand and compare the variety of organisational responses it is suggested, at the risk of some over-simplification, that there might be six different levels or groups of activity in measures to combat discrimination and exclusion and improve the employment integration of immigrants and ethnic minorities, the final of the six being diversity management itself. The ILO anti-discrimination training typology had been provided before the ILO research on anti-discrimination training had taken place, and had been used to organise the gathering of cases. In contrast, the new typology is to be applied retrospectively to the practices within the case studies and examples already provided in the two EU reports. More importantly, it aims to serve as a device to help make sense of current and future developments in the area.[9] The six categories are as follows:

1. Training the immigrants/minorities
2. Making cultural allowances
3. Challenging racist attitudes
4. Combating discrimination
5. Equal opportunities policies with positive action
6. Diversity management/mainstreaming

1. Training the immigrants/minorities   The first level of activity consists of measures directed at immigrants themselves to assist in their integration into society. Formal training is provided for the immigrants to improve their education and skills, and to help them learn the language, culture and customs of the new society, and the appropriate ways of behaving, as well as how to operate in the labour market. This approach is consistent with a 'supply side' or 'human capital' interpretation of ethnic inequality.

2. Making cultural allowances   Here, allowances are made for specific religious or cultural needs of minority groups within the organisation, and some staff will be trained in cultural awareness, or leading multiethnic teams. Similarly, service providers such as social workers, teachers, doctors and nurses, come to realise that they must be informed about immigrant cultures, and that immigrants may have 'special needs' related to their ethnic background.

3. Challenging racist attitudes   The previous level was a straightforward 'multi-cultural' approach which does not take account of the issues of racism and discrimination. This third level works from the assumption that the main barrier to change is the attitudes of people, and so publicity and information campaigns or training to reduce peoples' prejudices or racist attitudes are introduced.

4. Combating discrimination   The next level sees attempts to produce changes in people's behaviour to be necessary, as well as trying to change people's attitudes. Indeed, some argue that changing behaviour should take priority over attempting to change attitudes. Measures could include the introduction of fair recruitment and selection procedures, and training on how to operate these, and how to comply with anti-discrimination legislation. It could also cover anti-harassment policies and training, and the introduction of disciplinary measures against racism and discrimination within the organisation. Addressing discriminatory behaviour in these ways is seen to be important in creating a 'level playing field' by removing unfair barriers to opportunity.

---

9   This academic typology has been subsequently further developed and refined for activist and policy use by Taran and Gächter (2003).

5. Equal opportunities policies with positive action   The next level is to use a combination of the above approaches in a general equal opportunities package. There might be an equal opportunities statement for the organisation, a handbook for employees setting out the policy's intentions and procedures, and a target, such as the long-term aim of reflecting the ethnic mix of the local population in the workforce. Often there will be monitoring of the ethnic background of the workforce. The positive action initiatives are those over and above the simple provision of equal treatment and the production of a 'level playing field' through removing discriminatory barriers. There is an argument that such measures are not enough if migrants are starting from very different and disadvantaged positions, sometimes because of the operation of racism and discrimination in the past. Positive action, like the stronger American version, affirmative action, recognises the existence of a sort of structural discrimination known as 'past-in-present discrimination' (Williams 2000) whereby the exclusion experienced historically by certain groups means that inequality of opportunity will continue even when current discrimination processes are removed.

Positive action goes further than equal treatment. Whereas equal treatment would mean treating people who apply for jobs without discrimination, positive action means, for example, making an extra effort to encourage groups who might not normally apply. Therefore, positive action is in fact doing something extra for previously excluded minorities, something not being done for the national majority. Positive action might include special recruitment initiatives, such as translating job advertisements into ethnic minority languages, placing advertisements in the ethnic minority press, or using statements to encourage applications from minorities. It might include helping immigrants and ethnic minorities compete for work on a more equal footing with others in the labour market by providing extra training relating to their specific needs. An increasingly used measure is that of mentoring. This is intended to increase the retention of minorities once they have been recruited into the organisation. However, positive action is not positive discrimination – it does not seek to give ethnic minorities more favourable treatment in competition for jobs, and it does not entail reducing standards.

Also under this heading we might include external community initiatives by companies, such as providing special training schemes for immigrant and ethnic minority youth in disadvantaged areas, or even supporting cultural programmes in such areas. The argument is that businesses which operate in Europe's metropolitan areas stand to lose out from the social consequences stemming from increasingly marginalised ethnic communities. 'Because they operate in social environments, companies have a keen interest in ensuring that such communities are stable and prosperous' (Stewart and Lindburgh 1997: 28).

6. Diversity management/mainstreaming   The most ambitious level is that of diversity management, which can include many or all of the elements of the other approaches and adds diversity philosophy and practice to this, mainstreamed in a whole-organisation approach. Following the distinction made by Thomas (see Chapter 1) we can divide this level into two stages. The first is the stage of *valuing diversity*, where there is a positive desire to work towards an ethnically mixed workforce and a recognition of the positive benefits that a diverse workforce can bring to the organisation. The second stage is that of *managing diversity* which goes further than this by actively managing the diverse mix of employees in ways to contribute to organisational goals and develop a heterogeneous organisational culture.

By taking examples of practices from the two European reports under each of these headings in turn we can gain further insights into the background context for diversity management in Europe:

1. Training the immigrants/minorities

It was noticeable that the largest number of policy components in the *Compendium* fell under this heading. Historically, in many countries training of the immigrants themselves was one the first policy initiatives to be adopted following the first years of post-World War II immigration. Generally this was training for newcomers, teaching them the language, introducing them to important legal or cultural aspects of the new society, or showing them how to operate in the labour market. It was assumed that this would facilitate the 'integration' of immigrants into society.

Although primary immigration to EU countries had ended a generation previously, there were still seen to be certain categories of 'newcomer' which could benefit from such training, such as refugees and people who arrived through marriage and family reunion. Indeed, Thyssen Stahl, the German steel company, provided courses in German as a foreign language for the wives of workers newly arrived in Germany. In Sweden, Stockholm City Council provided a range of extra training courses to further the integration of foreign workers. Employees with a foreign nursing education received training to enable them to work as qualified nurses in Sweden. A special ten week course in Swedish for hospital kitchen staff was related specifically to their working environment, and the course participants attended full-time with pay. A case which appeared in both the *Gaining from Diversity* and the *Compendium* report was that of the Swedish telecommunications company Telia, with its special training for unemployed white collar immigrants, in cooperation with the Stockholm County Labour Market Board. Amongst those taking part were unemployed systems analysts, computer engineers and economists, and the training corresponded to future employment requirements at the company. One of the aims was to increase the proportion of immigrants employed at the company, an aim in which it succeeded (Soininen and Graham 1997).

In the *Gaining from Diversity* report there are many other examples under this heading. One is Levi Strauss & Co. in Belgium which, together with the Antwerp Chamber of Commerce and its partners, initiated a programme with four other firms to provide language training on the shop floor to low-skilled migrant workers. A full time worker was hired to promote the project and to coordinate the start-up activities in the companies. The first programme offered 120 hours of language training to 36 low-skilled migrant workers. This included one hour of instruction during working hours, and one hour just before or after the change in shift, both of which were compensated in the form of wages or vacation time (Stewart and Lindburgh 1997: 22).

Other examples come from Denmark and the UK. In Copenhagen the union for hotel and restaurant workers cooperated with private sector employers, the employment administration, and some Danish schools for adult education and vocational training to set up a migrant training school. The school operated during the annual period of low activity in the branch, from the end of September to the beginning of April. The participants in the course, all union members, received three months of full-time instruction, including intensive Danish-language instruction, an introduction to Danish society (such as information on employment and unemployment rights), computer training, and guidance in occupational safety (Stewart and Lindburgh 1997: 22). In London a local agency helped companies address the under-representation of ethnic minorities at higher levels by organising a training and mentoring programme for ethnic minority personnel working at or below the level of junior management. By mid 1996 the programme had involved more than 200 participants from 22 companies (Stewart and Lindburgh 1997: 24).

Other training initiatives in *Gaining from Diversity* – such as the programme for McDonalds staff in Copenhagen who wish to become managers, or the skill enhancement for low qualified 'at risk' employees at Barriol et Dallière in France – did not specifically target people of immigrant origin but appear in the report because they involve a 'significant number' of them in the training. Similarly, the training for temporary workers at the Viangros food company in Belgium covered 'ethnic minorities and other disadvantaged groups', and the Antwerp Chamber of Commerce supported a project giving support to unemployed low-skilled individuals 50 per cent of whom were of migrant origin (Stewart and Lindburgh 1997: 27).

Training for established immigrants

However, most of the immigrant and immigrant-descended population of Europe are not newcomers. There is, nevertheless, training with another sort of emphasis which can be relevant for some of these, reflecting the fact that the post-war immigrant workers to Europe were from the start over-represented in certain limited areas of job and sector, and have from then on been affected by economic and organisational change. In the *Compendium* there were examples of training for this older and more established immigrant population, in two contexts. The first was where restructuring of the economy has led to the closure of old industries and created widespread unemployment amongst immigrant workers, who had been over-represented in these employment sectors. In Belgium, the closure of coal mines led to the unemployment of large numbers of immigrants. An electrocoating company which decided to recruit from among these immigrants organised a special training scheme in cooperation with a local agency which had been set up to help the unemployed. The training covered technical shop floor matters, language and intercultural cooperation, and was targeted disproportionately towards immigrants (Martens and Sette 1997).

The second example was where restructuring within a firm had adversely affected the existing immigrant workforce by requiring from them skills or language abilities which had not been needed before. A video manufacturing company in Austria found that an imperfect knowledge of German by its immigrant employees was beginning to be a problem after production was reorganised into work teams. The company initiated training to fit in with shifts, covering German with relevance to the workplace. This reduced the necessity of replacing the immigrants with workers having a better knowledge of German (Gächter 1997). In Germany, Thyssen Stahl, a steel company with around eight per cent 'foreign' employees, in collaboration with the local adult education centre, offered German language courses for employees of foreign origin with a basic knowledge of German and a desire to improve their German for work-related reasons.

Therefore, the provision of training specifically targeted at the immigrant/ minority population is still in some circumstances an important activity. However, a continuing problem in Europe has been the persistence of the assumption that this activity should constitute the major thrust of measures to combat racism and xenophobia. There are problems in over-emphasising the role of training of immigrants, or as seeing it as sufficient in terms of activities. An over-emphasis on training directed at immigrants/minorities carries with it the assumption that the problems they encounter are a result of their own deficiencies. Yet there is a great deal of evidence that well-educated migrants and ethnic minorities with no language problems at all suffer discrimination and exclusion from opportunities for which they are well qualified (Zegers de Beijl 2000).

2. Making cultural allowances

An example in this category is the Belgian electrocoating company which took a number of initiatives for the benefit of workers of Maghrebian origin wishing to observe certain religious practices – for example, those who wish to pray can withdraw to the changing rooms to do so during breaks. Also they can take a longer leave period in the summer months if they put in a request to do so. This arrangement was introduced in order to give them a chance to return to their countries of origin and spend some time there.[10] The German steel company Thyssen Stahl introduced intercultural training, including a course on 'leading multicultural teams'. There were also 'intercultural weekends' for employees of various nationalities and their partners to get to know each others cultures better, and Turkish in the form of introductory and intermediate/ advanced courses for German employees wishing to learn Turkish or deepen their knowledge of Turkish for job-related or personal reasons. The example quoted in 'Gaining from Diversity' under this heading was that of the McDonalds restaurants in France, which take the religious practices of their employees into consideration, such as adjusting the hours of Muslim employees during Ramadam.

3. Challenging racist attitudes

Examples here were generally classifiable (in terms of the earlier ILO categories) under the headings of Information Training/Cultural Awareness Training, rather than

---

10 Strictly speaking this is not making cultural allowances, but making allowances for migrant origin, but is still best categorised under this heading.

the more aggressively attitude-changing Racism Awareness Training. Under this heading comes some of the activities of Stockholm City Council, which provided a course 'Racism and Xenophobia at Work' for work supervisors and teachers from the health-care college, addressing prejudices and hostile attitudes and providing the opportunity to discuss xenophobia and racism (Soininen and Graham 1997). In Germany, a 'Living with Foreigners' campaign was started jointly by the German trade union and employers federations, the DGB and the BDA. This was targeted at around one million apprentices in German industry, using training packages and media materials aimed at countering attitudes of intolerance and xenophobia (Brüggemann and Riehle 1997). In Denmark, all the employees of the local municipality of Århus, Denmark's second largest city, were sent a newspaper 'På lige fod' (On an equal footing) which presented success stories of ethnic minorities employed in the Council, the positive benefits of working with others from different cultures, and so on (Wrench 1997b). From the 'Gaining from Diversity' report a campaign under this heading is that of the Volvo company in Sweden, which responded to a series of racist incidents by putting out an advertisement entitled 'What would Volvo be without immigrants?' This pointed out that Volvo owed much of its success to the 70 different nations represented in 30–40 per cent of its current workforce (Stewart and Lindburgh 1997: 31).

These practices are rooted in common assumptions, namely that the provision of this sort of information will help to reduce racist attitudes and thereby reduce resistance to employing migrants, and furthermore that this attitude change will lead to changes in behaviour and discriminatory practices. However, some people question whether these assumptions are entirely defensible or whether the practices are adequate in themselves. For one thing, racist attitudes and prejudices are unlikely to be changed merely by the provision of information. Secondly, it is quite possible for practices of racial discrimination to be carried out by someone who does not have racist attitudes. From the previously mentioned European Foundation study (Wrench 1996) came examples of discrimination which cannot be categorised simply as a result of 'racist attitudes' on the part of particular gatekeepers. For example, in the UK there were employers who saw Indians as ambitious potential entrepreneurs not to be recruited for a particular job 'because they would go off and start their own business'. Some employers would refuse to recruit ethnic minorities because of the feared negative reaction of other people, such as clients, or the existing workforce. There were employers whose apparently neutral institutional practices indirectly operated to disproportionately exclude people from an ethnic minority background. These three different types of discrimination, labelled respectively 'statistical' 'societal' and 'indirect' discrimination (Williams 2000) cannot simply be categorised as resulting from conventional racist attitudes on the part of the individual carrying out the discrimination (See Chapter 6).

4. Combating discrimination

Therefore, for some practitioners, activities with the aim of producing changes in people's *behaviour* are more important than measures which are trying to change peoples' attitudes. Two examples of this kind of training which appeared in both the *Compendium of Good Practice* and the *Gaining from Diversity* report were that of Thyssen Stahl in Germany, which instructs personnel managers on how to base their recruitment and promotion criteria on principles of equal treatment and how to avoid inappropriate criteria for judgement, and the Belgian anti-discrimination code of conduct for the temporary employment agency sector. The latter was signed by employers and trade unions in that sector after a survey of agency staff had revealed that most had received discriminatory requests from employers (Martens and Sette 1997). These ranged from requesting perfect bilingualism for manual occupations – regarded as a kind of secret code for the exclusive selection of Belgian workers – to explicit requests not to be sent any foreigners. Both trade union and employers' representatives admitted that the temporary employment sector was beset with problems of racial discrimination. The training aimed to make staff aware of the problem of racial discrimination, and instructed them how to respond to employers who made discriminatory requests, and how to ensure that only functionally relevant requirements are taken into account when selecting temporary staff. Other examples of training which aimed to change practices of discrimination rather than change attitudes included the cases of a major British High Street retailer (Virdee 1997) and a Dutch public sector organisation (Abell 1997), both of which introduced training courses for staff who sit on recruitment and selection panels to help them avoid ethnic discrimination and bias in their procedures.

Sometimes unnecessary language requirements can be a form of indirect discrimination. In the 'Gaining from Diversity' report the Swedish company AGA reported that it no longer screened out applicants on the basis of poor language skills, but instead looked for other languages and special skills. With regard to tackling more direct forms of racial discrimination, KLM in the Netherlands appointed eight employees as *confidantes* for complaints regarding racial discrimination. Any employee who wished to discuss discrimination or make a complaint could contact one of these, and there was a 24 hour telephone number which explained the procedure and gave the telephone numbers of the *confidantes*. In London, Barclays Bank provided an information booklet for dealing with racial harassers, including informal methods – how to reply, how to document incidents – and formal methods, such as filing a formal grievance procedure (Stewart and Lindburgh 1997: 27).

5. Organisational equal opportunity policies with positive action

A British high street retailer, Virgin Our Price (Virdee 1997) and a Dutch public sector organisation, the North Holland Department of Public Works and Water Management (Abell 1997) both operated what might be called an equal opportunities policy at the whole-organisational level. Management at the British retailer introduced a policy against racial harassment, which stated that a single serious incident of harassment could result in summary dismissal for gross misconduct. The two organisations also introduced a series of measures which can be called 'positive action'. The British retailer carried out an audit of the workforce, and this showed that although the proportion of ethnic minorities employed was broadly in line with the size of the ethnic minority population nationally (just over 5 per cent), ethnic minorities were under-represented in middle management and senior positions. As part of the company's commitment to 'redressing past disadvantage through the adoption of positive action measures', it made special efforts to ensure that opportunities were made known to those groups, and where appropriate that training is provided to enable members of those groups to compete on equal terms for the opportunities available. (The law in the UK allows for an employer to provide in-service 'positive action' training for members of one particular racial or ethnic group to equip them for work in an area for which they are under-represented – Taylor 2000).

The Dutch public sector organisation was a department of public works responsible for flood defences and water management, traffic, transport and communications. The department is located within a highly multi-ethnic part of the Netherlands, and the head of personnel believed that this should be reflected in the workforce. Extra wording was added to recruitment advertisements to the effect that, all other things being equal, priority would be given to ethnic minorities, as well as to women and disabled people. To stimulate applications, contacts were then initiated with migrant organisations, and agreements were concluded with local temporary employment agencies that requests for temporary staff would be met in the first instance by candidates from one of the ethnic minorities. Preliminary interviews were held with applicants of minority ethnic origin where information was given about the organisation and the procedure, and how to improve letters of application and CVs. During selection, personnel officers were careful to see that the correct procedures were followed in the case of applicants of minority ethnic origin and that no improper arguments were used to reject them, and line managers underwent training in selection skills to avoid bias in selection interviews. Like the UK retailer, this organisation monitored the ethnic composition of its workforce over time. This practice allowed both the British and Dutch organisations to review their progress and make appropriate policy changes, and indeed, the monitoring was able to demonstrate that they had progressed significantly towards their long term targets of greater representation of ethnic minorities amongst their employees.

There is no description in *Gaining from Diversity* of a case study which could be categorised under this heading, with a fully-developed organisational equal opportunities policy and all its component levels of action. Whilst KLM in the Netherlands set a 12 month goal of placing 50 long-term unemployed into company vacancies, this was not positive action solely for ethnic minorities. The 'Gaining from Diversity' report does list many initiatives under the heading of 'external practices' by public and private sector employers. Examples were companies providing training for immigrant and ethnic minority young people who live in disadvantaged areas, or giving advice or assistance to ethnic minority-owned small businesses, as well as developing business partnerships with them.

6. Diversity management

The only case of an openly embraced organisational diversity management philosophy in the two reports is AB Volvo in Göteborg, Sweden, which had a policy of instituting diversity management throughout the various Volvo corporations. One programme included multicultural training for employees, efforts to include more work opportunities in the firm for immigrants, and adding diversity as part of the criteria for evaluating the quality of operations. The diversity commitment was set out in Volvo's corporate philosophy:

> Volvo is a global organisation with different cultures from all parts of the world. Involving people from other parts of the Group is an excellent way to gain strength, build confidence and develop networks. We will seek new paths by working in groups with co-workers who have different backgrounds and skills, across national borders. Internal mobility will be developed in order to broaden competence, to the benefit of both the Group and the individuals in it (Stewart and Lindburgh 1997: 26).

Implications for diversity management

If we look at both these reports together, we can attempt some generalisations on the state of organisational policies in this field in Europe towards the end of the 1990s which are relevant to understanding the development of diversity management in the European context. Both of these reports consisted of examples and case studies of 'good practice' which were selected by researchers to act as models for others to follow. We should recognise that these are somewhat imperfect indicators of practice, as the selection of cases in each case is a subjective exercise, not based on any sort of sample base, and not pretending to be a representative overview. Nevertheless, they were chosen by researchers who were looking for the best examples of good practice in this field and so we can assume that they do present a reasonable indication of what was seen as good practice operated by employers at this time.

In the case of each of the two reports, some of the examples have been disregarded in this analysis. Some in the Compendium have been omitted because they were not organisational case studies, but were national campaigns or agreements. From the 'Gaining from Diversity' several cases could not be included in this analysis because they described only the intention of their policy – e.g. that they would attempt to mirror the local population in their workforce – but without giving any detail as to the methods as to how this would be achieved. Allowing for the fact that some case studies appeared in both reports, then we are left with roughly 30 organisational cases, divided evenly between the two reports.

Thirty case studies

These 30 cases ranged from straightforward training schemes to the more ambitious multi-faceted policies at an organisational level. The main fact which stands out from these two exercises is the fact that, taken together, fully half of all the cases have as their primary activity practices which fall under the heading of the first category in the typology, 'training the immigrants/minorities'. This is consistent with the fact that within the public discourse on the integration of immigrants in EU countries in the 1990s there was a dominant focus on the human capital resources of the immigrant populations and their descendants, to the relative neglect of structural factors of exclusion such as discrimination. The assumptions behind this approach continue in public and media debate today, namely that 'integration problems' of immigrants will be solved by a largely one-way process of assimilation, facilitated by training. The distribution and emphasis of the cases which feature in both the European Foundation 'Compendium of Good Practice' and the 'Gaining from Diversity' report can be said to reflect this assumption that measures to promote equal treatment in the labour market are to be directed at the migrants themselves.

Under the second heading of 'making cultural allowances' there was one case where this was the primary activity, and five or six more where such actions were part of broader policies. In just four cases did policies include something which could be categorised under the third heading, 'challenging racist attitudes'. Another six had policies which could be described primarily as 'combating discrimination'. Of the final two categories of activity, – the more ambitious, organisational-level, equal opportunity policies with positive action, and diversity management – there were rather few examples. Whereas in a couple of cases there were activities which could be described as 'positive action', these were not part of a broader organisational equal opportunities policy. We can categorise just four cases from the two reports as proper organisational equal opportunities or diversity policies. Of these, two are Dutch, one British and one Swedish. In the *Compendium* there was no evidence of a diversity management awareness, although, by the criteria in our six-fold typology, two of the case studies were getting very close to what might be called a diversity management philosophy. In the 'Gaining from Diversity' report only one of the case studies used the language of diversity management. Thus, whilst the report accurately identified employers who were *Gaining from Diversity* it could not be described as a report of cases of 'Gaining from Diversity *Management*' according to the distinction made in Chapter 1. An added point of significance is that in the case of the Compendium of Good Practice, it was difficult for researchers in some of the EU countries to find any examples at all which they could categorise as 'good practice' against discrimination and integrating immigrants into employment. Indeed, it is quite likely that the biggest category would be a seventh one, at the very beginning of the list: '0 – doing nothing at all'.

Implications of the initiatives

There are a number of implications stemming from the examination of the four European initiatives of the 1990s for our concern with the later development of diversity management in Europe. The Joint Declaration uses exhortations to employers to use a range of activities which can be categorised as 'anti-discrimination', 'equal opportunities' and 'positive action'. These activities can also constitute many of the elements of a diversity management policy, and to justify these the Joint Declaration draws on a range of arguments associated also with a diversity management approach. However, it does not use the language of diversity management or talk explicitly about 'managing for diversity' as a strategy. In this sense the Joint Declaration was 'pre-diversity management', reflecting activities up to level 5 in the typology.

In the years immediately following the Joint Declaration came the three other initiatives within which we can identify the first signs of development of diversity management policies in some countries. The ILO anti-discrimination training study was applied in only five countries, but there was enough variety of experience in these five to enable us to raise some questions for future consideration. If the review of anti-discrimination training enables us to generalise more broadly about anti-discrimination activities in general, we can say that in some countries the awareness of any need for anti-discrimination measures was low, in some there was even positive hostility to the very notion of such measures, and that in other countries where anti-discrimination activities do exist there is evidence of different approaches and emphases. These observations, it was suggested, could have implications for the future spread of diversity management and the character of its content. The study did indicate signs of the adoption of diversity management in some EU countries.

The two European compendia of examples of good practice gave further impetus to these questions. In contrast to the advice of the Joint Declaration, which exhorted companies to adopt, (according to the typology) elements of levels 4 and 5 activities, supported by some of the arguments associated with level 6, the primary emphasis of the cases in both of the reports can be categorised as level 1 – training the immigrants. If we assume that diversity management, which can have a broad sweep, can in theory embrace elements from all six of these levels, then one question to ask is whether diversity management polices, which are now spreading more widely, will tend to reflect the 'supply side' bias and concern themselves with skills training for under-represented minorities rather, than, for example, measures to address the structures and cultures of exclusion within the organisations themselves.

Application of the typology

Broadly speaking, these pan-European exercises of the 1990s raise the question as to whether the acceptability, character and content of diversity management will reflect these already existing 'pre-diversity management' differences. The typology has been suggested as a device to help us monitor this. Typologies are useful for facilitating international comparisons. They stem from both theoretical reflection and empirical evidence, and the interaction between them. In this section we have suggested a new typology drawing on the albeit rather limited evidence of existing comparative work in the 1990s. The six-fold categorisation of organisational activities is an attempt to classify certain clusters of activities which have some internal consistency with each other and some theoretically significant differences from activities in other clusters.

Inappropriate categorisation

The typology can enable us to examine critically activities which take place under the headings of diversity management and related activities, and come to a closer understanding of their significance. For example, one question is whether some activities are mis-classified as diversity management, when according to the typology they are more appropriately classified as something else. We can illustrate this from one example, in this instance a Norwegian case which came to notice in 2000, at an international workshop on diversity management. Norway is an example of a country which until recently has had very little tradition of organisational polices on racial discrimination or employment equity. Then, in April 1999 a number of companies and interested parties came together and decided to set up a network and establish a 'competence centre', under the title of 'Mangfold i Arbeidslivet' (Diversity at the Workplace).[11] In the following year, at an international workshop on the subject, a Norwegian company set out its 'experiences of managing diversity'. This was an organisation of 500 employees with about 20 per cent of its production and warehouse workers coming from a minority ethnic background. The 'Managing for Diversity' initiative it described consisted of the following practices. Firstly, the company provided courses in the Norwegian language, tailored to issues in the working environment, and 50 per cent of which were allowed to take place in working hours. The second element was the recognition that the food provided on company training programmes and union courses should not, for example, include pork if Muslim or Jewish workers were to attend. A third initiative was to allow non-European workers to take extra unpaid leave for certain holiday periods so as to give them more time to spend on visits to their countries of origin. Finally, the company reported that it had been suggested that an activity for the future should be to hold some sort of meeting with Norwegian workers who have expressed negative attitudes to ethnic minorities, in order to try to neutralise these phenomena.

The company describes itself as having been 'working with diversity' for many years, and categorises its experiences as 'managing diversity'. However, if we use the typology to classify this company, we can say that it is not at the level 6 'diversity management' stage, properly defined. The policies it describes cover levels 1 and 2 in the typology, and show the first signs of awareness of a need to move into level 3. This example illustrates a relatively loose use of the term diversity management, a usage which is in danger of becoming increasingly common in Europe, particularly in contexts where little similar in terms of organisational policies has been experienced beforehand.

A chronology?

The Norwegian example leads us to a further question: does the typology consist of more than a list of categories but actually constitute a sequence of chronological stages, which are likely to be passed through over time? There is a logic which suggests that this could be so, at least in some countries. For example, level 1, training the immigrants, seems to be the first 'common sense' reaction in an immigrant receiving society when ethnic inequalities are perceived. When a 'supply side conscious' gives way to the idea that perhaps the majority institutions themselves should adapt, then level 2, 'making cultural allowances' comes relatively easily to mind. 'Culture' is something which is reasonably visible and some organisational responses to it can be

---

11 European Business Network for Social Cohesion 'Gaining from Diversity' Newsletter No. 3, May 1999.

made relatively painlessly. Then at some stage a 'multi-cultural' awareness transforms into an 'anti-racism' awareness, level 3, with the recognition that racism exists in societies, and probably also does in the organisation, and that multicultural approach does not address this source of exclusion. Thus training programmes are provided for what is probably assumed to be the minority of workers with racist attitudes or ethnic prejudices. A more ambitious leap of imagination is called for in order to get to the anti-discrimination stage, partly because this entails the more uncomfortable recognition that racial discrimination can exist 'normally' in organisations and can be perpetrated by ordinary people who are not conventionally classifiable as having racist attitudes or prejudices. Another reason why this level might take longer to be accepted is that it entails some changes in organisational routines and practices, rather than the more superficial approach in the preceding level, such as simply running training courses or educational campaigns against racism. The level of equal opportunity policies with positive action calls for a more ambitious development of consciousness, not only because it is a more ambitious policy in terms of the range of activities, but also because the acceptance of positive action implies the recognition of the existence of forces of structural or historical discrimination, and the corresponding recognition that simply providing a level playing field through the removal of barriers of discrimination will not be enough. Finally the diversity management level is the most ambitious of all because by definition it addresses the whole organisation itself, implies major changes in organisations practices and culture, and is adopted first at the senior management level.

The chronology of this typology is in fact consistent with one observation on the historical trend of policy approaches to ethnic diversity and labour market participation in the Netherlands (Nimako 1998, cited in Essed 2001). When studying policies relating to Amsterdam South-East, the most ethnically diverse area in the Netherlands, Nimako identifies a trend in Dutch policies through four historical paradigms: *deficit* (shortcomings in minority ethnic groups which need to be compensated for), *difference* (cultural difference is the main determinant of the positioning of newcomers), *discrimination* (a central problem is the forces of exclusion of those perceived as ethnically or racially different) and *diversity* (inclusiveness and valuing differences are important for organisational advantage). The Dutch example suggests that a chronological move through the levels of the typology is at least feasible and can be reflected in reality.

The use of a typology like the one above should serve as a device to categorise and clarify different activities in different EU contexts. But it may allow consideration of a more theoretically interesting question too. If we can identify significant clusters of activities at the different levels within the content of diversity management and related polices in different member states, we may want to speculate on the extent to which these differences are related to variables of national context. Furthermore, do these national differences imply that a common trajectory through the six different levels towards diversity management cannot be taken for granted? The question of what might constitute these significant variables of national context is addressed in the next section.

Chapter 4

Convergence and Constraints in European Diversity Practice

Since the comparative work of the 1990s, described in Chapter 3, there is evidence that a diversity management consciousness has been spreading more widely in Europe. In the UK there were in the 1990s a number of initiatives which provided a sympathetic context for the move in the direction of diversity management. One was the 'Race for Opportunity' campaign, launched in October 1995 'to encourage business to invest in the diversity of Britain's ethnic minority communities' and enhance their competitiveness by creating 'an inclusive management environment'. The Race for Opportunity newsletter has been full of stories of diversity activities and projects of major companies all over the UK, and activities such as the annual Award for Excellence in Diversity. A 1997 initiative by the UK's Commission for Racial Equality (CRE) called the 'Leadership Challenge' aimed to get Britain's leaders to declare their commitment to the principles of diversity and racial equality and the practices to work towards these. By May 1998 the leaders of 178 companies and organisations had signed up to the 'Challenge'. Following this came 'Race for the Future', an initiative of the Department for Education and Employment, 'aimed at taking the message to employers that racial equality in the workforce is essential for good business practice', through regional conferences aimed at local business leaders, and other events. In 1999 the Stephen Lawrence Inquiry report[1] (Macpherson 1999) raised questions about racism in public organisations, and provided a stimulus for many public organisations and local authorities to review their equal opportunity and anti-racism procedures and to develop new initiatives. Following the Inquiry report, the government introduced the Race Relations (Amendment) Act 2000, which places a new general statutory duty on public authorities, (e.g. local councils, central government departments, schools, colleges, universities and health authorities) to monitor by ethnic group their existing staff as well as applicants for jobs, promotion and training. Authorities with at least 150 full-time staff must also monitor other things such as disciplinary action, grievances, training and dismissals.[2]

The Chartered Institute for Personnel and Development is the leading professional association in the UK for personnel and human resource managers, and sees itself as 'the pre-eminent professional body influencing and improving the quality, thinking and practice of people management and development.' It is therefore significant in

---

1 An inquiry into the actions of the police following the murder of the black teenager Stephen Lawrence, and the subsequent mishandling of the case by the public authorities, which meant that his murderers were never convicted.

2 *Connections* Autumn 2001 p. 6 (CRE London).

the UK context that this body has thrown its weight behind diversity management. In a 1998 publication *Managing Diversity: an IPD position paper* it strongly asserts its commitment to diversity management and sets out how and why British companies should adopt it. In 1999 a survey was carried out of the top 200 British companies, selected from the Financial Times 500. One third of those who responded were actively involved in the management of diversity,[3] with a further 12 per cent of the remainder reporting that they were planning to do something in this area over the next 12 months (Collet and Cook 2000). Those organisations which were involved in managing diversity were more likely to be involved in nation-wide campaigns such as Race for Opportunity and the CRE's Leadership Challenge. This survey illustrated the beginning of a diversity management consciousness in the UK, but also indicated that it was still a minority activity. As the authors themselves stated, bearing in mind that the people who took part in the survey were from companies, where an emphasis on diversity is more likely to be found, it could reasonably be assumed that the overall proportion of British organisations committed to diversity at that time was much lower than one-third. (Collet and Cook 2000: 6). However, over the next five years the Race for Opportunity network demonstrated a noticeably growing receptiveness to racial equality and diversity policies amongst its own member organisations, as indicated in its annual benchmarking report of 113 private and public sector organisations' policies. Whereas in 2001 38 per cent of member organisations could identify a clear business case for racial equality, by 2005 this had risen to 91 per cent (*Equal Opportunities Review* 144, August 2005: 4). A minority but growing trend is for a company to require its suppliers to have good diversity practices. One of the UK's largest companies, Barclays, is requiring the law firms which give it legal advice to provide diversity information, and a major employment charity, The Shaw Trust, warned its suppliers in 2006 that their contracts depended on their demonstration of an active diversity and equality policy (*Equal Opportunities Review* No. 151, April 2006/ No. 153, June 2006)

In the Netherlands the government introduced a number of specific labour market measures to promote the employment of ethnic minorities. An agreement in 2000 meant that the employers' organisation for small and medium sized businesses had to report 30,000 vacancies to the employment services authority, to be 'preferably' filled by persons from ethnic minorities. An Act which came into force in 1998 pressed employers with 35 or more employees to reflect a proportional share of ethnic minorities in their workforces. And in 2000 an agreement was made between government ministers and a leading group of large companies on the implementation of a multicultural personnel policy which can include matching recruitment channels to a target group of ethnic minorities, introducing culture-free selection tests, providing intercultural management training to managers and members of the works council, appointing mentors for newcomers, and so on (Ramkhelawan 2001). In 2004 the government set up the National Diversity Management Centre, where examples of good practice in diversity management are listed.[4] There has been a

---

3   Sixty-five completed questionnaires were returned, a response rate of just under one third.

4   www.div-management.nl.

long history in the Netherlands of intercultural management training, which in the 1980s directed itself reasonably easily into embracing the cultural minorities at work in the Netherlands, occupying an industry of training providers who ranged from professional management consultants to small ideologically motivated anti-racist voluntary organisations (Abell 1991). Many of these subsequently developed into diversity management trainers and consultants.

It seems that the first organisations to be interested in diversity issues in the Netherlands were those offering products or services to ethnic minority clientele, and multinationals companies who are operating in an international market. According to the one Dutch diversity consultant, at the time working on diversity management policies with Amsterdam City Council and the Dutch police force, in the early 2000s a diversity management consciousness was growing significantly in the Netherlands. One of the main stimuli to this was full employment, so that managers have been turning to diversity management out of a pressing need to recruit more people. In the experience of this consultant, the organisations which were most concerned about the positive effect that a diversity management policy can have on clients and customers were the banking and insurance industries, and these were often operating policies to match their workforces with the local area representation of minorities. The public sector organisations, on the other hand, were more likely to be concerned with the issue of staff shortages. In his opinion, all the major Dutch municipalities were now talking about diversity management.

In Sweden a new anti-discrimination law in 1999 put more pressure on employers to adopt anti-discrimination and diversity measures. The Swedish Discrimination Ombudsman produced a handbook on best practice to promote cultural diversity and was given the right to approach firms and check what they are doing to promote diversity. The new law allows some positive action in the area of recruitment and improving working conditions for ethnic minorities (EUMC 2001: 74). The Swedish government also pressed city councils and local authorities to do something in this area. The organisation 'Sweden 2000' has worked with diversity networks initiated by the Swedish Ministry of Industry in a range of initiatives to promote diversity in the workplace. Sweden 2000 has organised diversity workshops attended by delegates from both the private and public sector, and has also organised diversity study visits of representatives of Swedish companies to the US to meet diversity practitioners from American companies. In 2005 a market research agency, TEMO, carried out an investigation among small and medium-sized companies in Sweden, and found out that six out of ten had recruited during the previous three years 'with the intention of increasing diversity in the company', and that a majority were of the view that 'increased diversity should benefit the company's commercial opportunities'.[5]

One Swedish diversity management consultant[6] stated that people in Sweden first began talking about diversity management around 1995–96; it was the larger Swedish companies such as Telia and Volvo for whom it first became a major interest. She felt that relatively few Swedish companies were driven by a realisation that

---

5   Temo (2005) Mångfald i arbetslivet – En undersökning bland små och medelstora företag.

6   Personal interview March 2001.

there was an ethnic minority market to exploit. Nor did she think that the notion that 'diversity leads to creativity' was a driving force for diversity management. Instead she felt that the two main pressures were the realisation of present or future labour shortages, and a concern over company image. Broomé et al. (2000) came to similar conclusions after their interviews with Swedish employers. They found no evidence of the view that making use of immigrants' cultural, social or linguistic experience could benefit the company or enhance the quality of service, or enrich the workplace environment for the native Swedish employees. Indeed, their interviews with people in the public sector found that the motives for employing immigrants were those such as meeting the labour shortage, and that better services can be provided to immigrants themselves, avoiding the need for extra interpreters, and so on. 'The internal organisational advantages of a diverse workforce are hardly given any prominence in the interviews' (p. 28). Thus it would seem that by the early 2000s, both in the Netherlands and Sweden, there were pressures which were stimulating a diversity management consciousness, but it also seems that in both countries the full potential of the diversity management philosophy had not yet been embraced.

In Denmark in 1998 a number of human resource managers from several large businesses established an organisation called 'Foreningen Nydansker'.[7] The aim was to improve the employment integration of 'new Danes' and highlight the potential and qualifications of immigrants and ethnic minorities in Denmark. More than 150 public and private sector companies and organisations signed up as members. The organisation organised conferences and workshops focusing on new Danes and the labour market and established cooperative working links with unions, employers associations, public authorities, and others. The director and a team of volunteer human resource managers made themselves available to disseminate the message of diversity management and give advice to companies on the recruitment and employment of new Danes. According to the director, the first to take on board the message were the large companies, international companies, and American-owned businesses. In 2001 the organisation produced a report which brought together examples of good practice from companies and organisations all over Denmark, to serve as models for others.[8] One major Danish pharmaceutical company, Novo Nordisk, announced in 2001 its plans for 'working actively with equal opportunities', including setting a target for each affiliate and unit to develop an action plan for addressing equal opportunities. The company argued 'Diversity should be seen not as a problem, but as an opportunity. Creating a corporate culture that supports diversity will be vital to securing equal opportunities for all'.[9]

The fact that Ireland has only recently become a country of immigration has stimulated attention in diversity management issues rather later than some others. In 2005 Fáilte Ireland, the official Irish Tourism body, launched its strategy of 'Cultural Diversity' aimed at the effective management of an increasingly culturally diverse

---

7   The full title is 'Foreningen til integration af nydanskere på arbejdsmarkedet' which means the association for the integration of new Danes (immigrants) into the labour market.

8   'Ledelse af mangfoldige ressourcer – integration of nydanskere på arbejdspladsen'.

9   'Reporting on the Triple Bottom Line 2001: Dealing with Dilemmas' Novo Nordisk, Bagsværd 2001.

workforce.[10] Similarly the Irish Health Service Employers Agency has developed guidance for managers on how diversity might best be accommodated in the workplace.

A number of European initiatives (for example both Sweden 2000 and Foreningen Nydansker) had links with the Centre for Diversity and Business in London, which saw its mission as being one of highlighting the importance of diversity to the economic and social development of Europe, and 'show how creating and managing diversity in all its forms will be vital to the competitiveness of Europe in the next 20 years'. From its website in the early 2000s could be seen links to diversity activities elsewhere in Europe. There was a project with the Finnish Ministry of Labour, the University of Jyväskylä and several major companies in the development of a programme to develop the diversity skills of managers and staff in Finland. There was a link with a Norwegian network with the title of 'Mangfold i Arbeidslivet' (Diversity at the Workplace), set up in 1999 by a number of companies and interested parties who came together to further diversity initiatives in Norway. In Belgium it reported on employers' groups and networks which became involved in campaigns to raise awareness of the business benefits of diversity and disseminate good practice accordingly. In Italy it referred to Sodalitas, which, following on from the European Business Network for Social Cohesion initiative 'Gaining from Diversity', set up a task force in 1998 composed of people from industry, the professions, and social and voluntary agencies.

Two European Commission reports

Whilst by the end of the 1990s there were noticeable strands of development in the direction of diversity management, this was clearly still a minority activity in EU countries. Two subsequent reports by the European Commission provided further insight into European developments. In 2003 the European Commission published a report entitled *The Costs and Benefits of Diversity*, a study on the methods and indicators to measure the cost-effectiveness of diversity policies in enterprises (European Commission 2003). This investigation included a survey of 200 companies in four EU countries, and eight case studies of diversity initiatives in six EU countries. The report concluded that the 'business case' for investment in workplace diversity in Europe is somewhat fragmented and at an earlier stage of development than in, for example, the US and Canada, but that 'a potentially powerful case for investment in workforce diversity policies is beginning to emerge'.

Two years later came a second report by the Commission *The Business Case for Diversity: Good Practices in the Workplace,* published in 2005. The aim was to select and analyse successful and innovative examples of good practice in diversity management implemented by employers and businesses across the European Union, as 'part of the Commission's ongoing efforts to promote diversity in the workplace and combat discrimination across the enlarged European Union' (European Commission

---

10 Fáilte Ireland, (2005). *Cultural Diversity. Strategy and Implementation Plan*, available at: www.failteireland.ie.

2005: 9). Two surveys were made of companies in 25 EU Member States, producing a total 919 responses. The first survey used the European Business Test Panel (EBTP) to administer an on-line questionnaire to investigate diversity awareness and practices of member companies across all areas of diversity. The EBTP is a panel of around 3000 businesses from 25 EU Member States, plus Norway, which is designed to be statistically representative of businesses throughout the Union. The questionnaire was circulated to around 3000 panellist companies, and generated 798 responses, a 26.6 per cent return.

The responses give some clues as to the state of diversity awareness and diversity management practice across EU Member States in the middle of the first decade of the 21st century. Almost half of all the EBTP survey businesses that responded to the survey were actively engaged in promoting workplace diversity and integration. Of all the business benefits of diversity policies, one of the most important was reported to be resolving labour shortages and recruiting and retaining high quality staff. Among the 798 respondents of the EBTP survey it was the single highest scoring benefit. It was also evident from the case study examples that internal diversity was leading to marketing and product developments that cater for new market segments.

The second survey used questionnaires and in-depth interviews to identify examples of good practice in workplace diversity in the areas of 'race' and ethnicity, age, sexual orientation, disability, and religion or belief. An initial questionnaire was sent to around 3000 contacts across Europe, covering companies of various sizes and from different industrial sectors. The questionnaire invited them to participate in the research and submit their diversity initiatives. A total of 121 submissions from companies were received. Then 58 companies with promising practices were invited to complete a more detailed questionnaire outlining their diversity initiative. Following this, on-site visits and interviews were conducted with 28 companies to get additional information about their diversity practices. The authors of the report concluded that companies are making 'steady progress' in the implementation of diversity and equality policies in Europe.

Of course there are limitations to the degree to which the EBTP survey can be seen as 'representative', because those who responded were probably more likely to be those with diversity management policies in the first place. But it does provide a further indication of the growing awareness of the subject in European business, and it can also give a suggestion of the countries in which it is most and least common. For example, it is noticeable that countries from Southern Europe accounted for only seven per cent of the replies. Similarly, regarding the second 'good practice' survey, most of the 121 submissions came from the member states of northern Europe in the 'old' EU15. Of the named participating companies, as set out in the Annex to the report, the largest number, almost a third, came from the UK. The next largest numbers in EU countries came from Spain, Germany and Belgium, followed by France, the Netherlands and Sweden. In general the level of responses and good practice submissions received from companies based in the ten new EU member states and from southern Europe was relatively low. It is also noticeable that most corporate diversity initiatives were still focused mainly on gender equality issues. Of the 19 examples which appeared in the report as case studies, less than half included ethnicity as one of the criteria of the policy. Five of the 19 case studies came from the UK, and four of these five covered ethnicity, whilst none of the three German cases did.

In 2003 Point and Singh carried out an analysis of statements on the websites of 241 'top' companies in eight European countries – Finland, France, Germany, the Netherlands, Norway, Sweden, Switzerland and the UK – in order to see if they used the word 'diversity', and how they defined it. Companies in the UK were the most likely to show a commitment to diversity on their websites, with nearly all of the top 50 companies doing so. Of the other EU countries, just over half the German companies did, followed by the French and Dutch with over a third, and the Swedish with just under a third. The lowest proportion was found in Finland, with one fifth. The most frequently cited dimension of the policies was that of 'gender', followed by 'culture'. French and German companies used the broader notion of 'culture' whilst UK companies referred instead to 'race and ethnicity' (Point and Singh 2003: 756).

Encouragement measures

Thus the limited but increasing information from a number of surveys suggests a growing but rather 'patchy' development of diversity management in Europe. In this context, a number of initiatives for encouraging employers have developed, both at a national and EU level (EUMC 2004, 2005, 2006a). For example, in Belgium in December 2005, approximately fifty employers (representing almost 150,000 employees) active in the Brussels-Capital Region signed a 'Charter for Diversity'. In 2005, the Interministerial Conferences on integration and employment developed a new instrument to promote equality in the labour market, the 'diversity trademark', to be awarded to companies in Belgium that can clearly demonstrate the practical ways they promote diversity within and outside their organisation. This is similar to the MIA prize for diversity in Denmark, instituted in 2003 and now awarded annually to companies by the Danish Institute for Human Rights (Nour and Thisted 2005: 19). Also in Belgium, in 2005 the *Cel Kleurrijk ondernemen/Cellule entreprise multiculturelle* [Unit colourful enterprising] was created in the Federal Administration to persuade and advise employers and company directors on how to develop diversity management in their companies. In the same year a comparable organisation was set up for the federal public sector, the *Cel Diversiteit/Cellule Diversité* [Unit on Diversity], responsible for the implementation of the Diversity Action plan 2005–2007. An encouragement measure from Ireland is the project DAWN, the Diversity at Work Network[11] whose objective is to help local business communities to create an 'intercultural environment' in the workplace that targets minority ethnic workers, and develop a 'whole organisation' approach to diversity policies. According to the Centre for Diversity and Business, an Italian management training institute set up a project in Italy called 'Diversity Management', financed partly with European Union money, to promote initiatives in Italian organisations with regard to new problems of cultural diversity. There are also encouragement measures at EU level. For example, the European Commission runs an EU-wide

---

11 Equal Community Initiative in Ireland, http://www.equal-ci.ie.

campaign 'For Diversity – Against Discrimination' in order to raise awareness and stimulate debate on diversity issues.

From the evidence above it seems reasonable to conclude that there is an expanding though patchy development of activities in the direction of diversity management. There is a growth in Europe in 'diversity consciousness' even though, strictly speaking, much of it does not yet look like a diversity *management* consciousness, and some of these activities labelled diversity management might be more correctly categorised elsewhere on the earlier six-fold typology of organisational activity.

A European convergence towards diversity management?

In the light of the steady spread of awareness and activities under the broad heading of diversity, it is relevant to ask whether there are forces that will produce a convergence of organisational practice across Europe towards diversity management. Certainly some diversity management practitioners and consultants have an almost evangelical faith in the power of the new diversity gospel to spread into untouched areas. Of course, one factor in such a convergence within the EU might be the pressure which stems from the mechanisms of the European Union itself. More particularly, the EU anti-discrimination directives, one on equal treatment of people irrespective or race or ethnic origin (the Racial Equality Directive) and one establishing a general framework for equal treatment in employment and occupation (the Employment Equality Directive) require the establishment and maintenance of a minimum level of protection against discrimination in employment. The directives were adopted in 2000 and needed to be transposed by the 15 EU member states by 2003, and by the new 10 member states by 2004.[12] As described in Chapter 3, EU member states needed to revise their existing laws or introduce new ones in line with the requirements of these directives. Furthermore, Article 13 of the Racial Equality Directive states that member states must designate a body to promote equal treatment, and to provide legal standing for relevant organisations to support victims of discrimination in pursuing their complaints. All this is likely to put pressure on employers to adopt anti-discrimination procedures themselves, and diversity management is likely to be seen as an acceptable way of doing this. Indeed, the authors of the European Commission's 2005 report *The Business Case for Diversity* conclude that it is reasonable to infer that recent EU antidiscrimination legislation has had a considerable impact in promoting action in this field.

However, more than this, there could be other factors which might be drawn upon to construct something like a universalist theory of convergence towards diversity management, operating regardless of national context. For a discussion of such universalist theoretical positions we can turn to the work of O'Reilly (1996), on theoretical considerations in cross-national employment research. O'Reilly points out that early 'universalist' social theorists such as Marx, Weber and Durkheim, despite coming from different political positions, shared similar basic assumptions

---

12 Regarding the Employment Equality Directive, there was an extended period for transposition in relation to its provisions on disability and age.

about the common trajectory of human development. Their unilinear model of social evolution was challenged by anthropologists such as Malinowski whose functional analysis of single societies showed that societies were unique coherent entities and implied that they needed to be understood from a more holistic approach. The key difference is indicated by O'Reilly, as being 'those who stress universal trends often underplay cultural differences in their search for similar patterns across societies, whilst those who stress divergence tend to take a more holistic approach and give a greater emphasis to the impact of culture' (O'Reilly 1996: 3). Therefore, this means that 'The concept of culture as a significant explanatory variable is a key concern in cross national comparative research.' The problem for social scientists engaged in comparative work is 'how to conceptualise and operationalise culture for empirical research'.

One universal theory of convergence is 'industrialism'. Industrialism seeks to identify universal trends in industrial organisation, emphasising, for example, a technological imperative which leads to a single trajectory of development. Thus, according to this theory, a logic of industrialism exists regardless of the political context (Kerr 1983). Similarly, contingency theory, which restricts its focus to business structures and organisations rather than whole societies, concentrates on, for example, differences in organisational design and practices in relation to factors like organisational size, the environment or the technology used (Woodward 1965, Lawrence and Lorsch 1967). These theories might have relevance for those who identify a 'convergence' towards diversity management. As described in Chapter 2, major external forces – globalisation, continuing post-industrial migration, demographic shifts, the decline of manufacturing and the growth of the service sector – could be seen as similar forces for convergence towards this particular form of managerial response. In the face of these 'irresistible' structural forces and pressures, firms will need to adopt diversity management techniques in order to survive.

However, universalist positions have been criticised for over-emphasising structural determinants and for underplaying the significance of local historical, cultural and political factors. As O'Reilly argues, even if organisations or societies experience comparable pressures it cannot be assumed that they will adopt identical strategies to deal with these because national institutions, coalitions of actors and values mediate the change process (O'Reilly 1996: 8).

Thus, despite the apparently universal pressures and imperatives identified as the key stimulants to the development of diversity management, it will be important to examine the development of this and other organisational anti-discrimination practices within national or local cultural and institutional contexts.

The variable of national culture

If within different EU countries we find clusters of differences in the character of the most common anti-discrimination activities – for example, if we find them characterised by different levels in the six-fold typology – we should ask the question as to whether this not so much because they are at different 'stages' in a chronological sequence of development but because the dominant activity reflects enduring differences in certain aspects of local or national culture, or in different local or national institutions. There have been many studies on the implications of national culture for management practice. For example, writers such as Hofstede (1991) argue that people of a particular nationality share a collective national culture, a sort of mental programming which shapes their values, attitudes, perceptions, behaviour and competences. Theories of organisations reflect the cultural environment from which they originate, so 'there can be no guarantees that management theories and concepts developed within the cultural context of one country can, with good effect, be applied in another' (Morden 1999: 20). However, there has been relatively little written so far on the specific implications of national culture for *diversity* management.[13] Within the human resource management and organisational literature there is an expanding interest in cross cultural aspects of organisational behaviour (Adler 1997). Questions are asked as to whether there is just one basic and universally applicable 'human resource management', or whether we should talk about a variety of nationally specific models (see Harzing and Van Ruysseveldt 1995, Clark 1996). The same question needs to be addressed with regard to diversity management. Are local or national culturally-rooted values a constraint on the development of diversity management?

For example, such a cultural constraint might be the 'particularism' which is characteristic of some parts of Europe. A family-based particularism is said to be common in areas such as the south of Italy, Greece and Spain, and is a phenomenon which is 'characterised by the elevation of family bonds above all other social loyalties' (Mutti 2000: 582). In a society where this carries through into organisational practices it will have implications for policies targeted to produce a more diverse workforce. For example, trade unions may have formal or informal agreements with employers which prioritise their own family members for jobs, and thereby exclude newcomers. In Nice, in the south of France, there was reported in the late 1990s an agreement between the trade unions and public transport employers that priority for all new jobs on the buses should go to the children of existing bus drivers. The bus company began to have problems on the buses with some young people of immigrant descent and decided that that the problem might be helped if they were to recruit some people of immigrant background. However, the trade union agreement initially made it difficult for the drivers to accept this new scheme to prioritise the recruitment of people of immigrant background, until eventually a new agreement was made which reserved 50 per cent of jobs for the family of drivers, and 50 per cent for external recruitment (Wrench 2000). This type of family priority in recruitment is a clear example of indirect discrimination, and is not compatible with an equal opportunities or diversity management policy.

Is this factor of particularism to be considered a trait of national culture in the sense used by Hofstede, with inevitable implications for organisational practices like diversity management? Or is there a danger of overstating the implications of such culturally-based value differences? Hofstede's work has been criticised as being rather too simplistic, in, for example, reducing the cultural identity of a society to

---

13 One textbook which does address US and European differences with regard to diversity management is Kirton and Greene 2000.

a standardised score based on individual responses to series of statements, ignoring conflicting identities which exist in societies, and underplaying the rate of historical change (O'Reilly 1996: 10). For example, in certain regions and industries in the UK there has also been a similar historical tradition of family priority in recruitment, but this type of tradition was fought against and removed by the political mobilisation within trade unions of ethnic minority workers. The fact that such prioritisation of family members has changed over 20 years from being considered 'normal' to being considered morally unacceptable was shown in the mid 1990s when the Transport and General Workers Union insisted that its drivers' section at Fords abandon such a policy even at the risk of alienating and losing 200 union members (Purkiss 1997). Clearly, values, traditions and associated practices can be affected by political action and can change over time. There is a danger in giving too great a determining role to values alone. When looking at any differences within the EU in organisational anti-discrimination practices we need to consider the interaction of a range of relevant variables. Certainly national culture or national value differences are likely to be among these variables, but these need also to be located in the context of social institutions. As O'Reilly puts it, values on their own are not enough to understand different working and organisational practices – 'Values need to be rooted into the social and economic structure of a given society' (O'Reilly 1996: 9). We need to observe how local or national cultural and value differences shift over time, and how they are reinforced, undermined or manipulated by political developments.

This chapter therefore suggests some examples of the sorts of institutional, cultural and political factors which may act as enablers or constraints on the development of American-style diversity management in Europe. There is insufficient space here to list all of the intra-European differences of culture, history and institutions which might have some relevance to diversity management, but we can consider a number which spring to mind as the sorts of factors which might be relevant. These national differences in variables relevant to the development of diversity management can be related to legal, cultural or political regularities within member states.

Differences of national context

There may be elements within some of the six levels of organisational anti-discrimination practice which make them less likely to find a sympathetic environment in various EU countries. For example, one central component of the practice of diversity management (level 6) is the identification and celebration of ethnic diversity at the workplace. Yet in some parts of Europe the very idea of this might be seen as unacceptable.

The example of France

Bourdieu and Wacquant, for example, criticise the 'cultural imperialism' inherent in the assumption that American academic ideas can be imposed on non-American environments. For them, an example of such 'cultural imperialism' is the American imposition of the word 'minority' with all its unstated assumptions and presuppositions that 'categories cut out from within a given nation-state on the basis of "cultural" or "ethnic" traits have the desire or the right to demand civic and political recognition as such' (Bourdieu and Wacquant 1999: 46, 51). For some people in France the very word 'diversity' has unacceptable overtones. The American historian Nancy Green, when describing the French discourse on immigration, notes that some French writers see that the US is no longer the immigration 'melting pot' it once claimed to be – they argue that 'the United States has renounced its literal melting pot to follow a dangerous path of diversity, which France should in no way copy' (Green 1999: 1199). The phenomenon in the US is summarised by Prasad and Mills (1997: 16) 'Today ethnicity is worn proudly as a badge of honour, (.....) preventing the easy assimilation of different ethnic groups into something loosely defined as American'. This is a development which would be seen as unacceptable by many in France. Green sums the French view up thus 'As seen from across the Atlantic, then: the melting pot is dead (in the United States) long live the melting pot (in France)' (Green 1999: 1204).

There are differences in the degree to which policies against racism and discrimination entail, as part of their approach, a practical recognition of ethnic categories. The French idea of its national community does not sit well with the recognition of ethnic or immigrant minorities within it.

> The principle of French policy is to be 'colour blind'. No 'minority' policies exist, nor the very idea of minorities. According to this approach, multiculturalism or ethnic cultures should remain in the private sphere, and should not be recognised in the public domain (Schnapper et al. 2003: 15).

Thus in France the emphasis is on broader 'equal rights' policies as a means of avoiding discrimination for all citizens and workers, and initiatives to encourage the recruitment of migrants have been phrased not in terms of 'anti-discrimination' or 'anti-racism' policies for migrants, but as egalitarian approaches guided by a universalistic ideology (De Rudder et al. 1995). To talk of measures in 'Anglo-Saxon' equal opportunities terms runs counter to established philosophies of universalistic treatment, with a resistance to dividing up the targets of policies by ethnic background. Therefore, in France, practices which benefit ethnic minorities are more likely to do so indirectly, without being designed in ethnically-specific forms. This contrasts with the British situation, where there is a much weaker and more complicated conception of citizenship and the national community, which has not been threatened by the recognition of ethnic categories or ideas of multiculturalism. Discussion on the forms that multiculturalism might take are a regular part of public debate in some sectors, and equal opportunities policies often operate in ways which take practical account of categories of ethnic difference (Jenkins and Solomos 1987, Blakemore and Drake 1996).

Differences in ethnic monitoring

It is clear that the French context is unsympathetic for some aspects of diversity management – level 6 – and also for some activities at level 5 – organisational equal opportunity policies with positive action. One important component of both these levels of activity is the audit – counting the ethnic origin of the organisations' workforce in order to identify discriminatory processes, and perhaps in order to use anti-discriminatory positive action measures such as setting targets to reflect the local ethnic mix in the workforce. As the International Personnel Management Association put it, when describing 'best practices' in diversity management in the US, 'Best practice organizations utilize workforce data and demographics to compare statistics reported for the civilian labor force. Occupations with under-utilization are identified and goals are established to reduce the under-utilization' (Reichenberg 2001: 2). However, in France the recording of 'racial' or ethnic origin in official or private registration runs strongly counter to social and legal norms.

It is not only France where there are problems of this sort. Even in the Netherlands, which is a country with one of the strongest records of equal employment opportunity and diversity management practices, there has been considerable opposition to the practice. In the context of a 1994 law that was being introduced to encourage the proportional labour market participation of ethnic minorities, a 'major bottleneck' turned out to be the issue of identification and registration. The chairman of one of the most influential employers' organisations stated that everyone with some awareness of what happened in the Second World War had to oppose any form of ethnic registration (Glastra et al. 1998: 170). A Swedish diversity management consultant described the discussion on ethnic monitoring and targets as something of a 'heated debate' in Sweden. Opponents in Sweden also draw on the argument 'What if the Nazis got hold of this?' She recognised that this reluctance gives rise to problems regarding diversity management in Sweden because of the fact that in the (US) diversity management literature, monitoring is quite important. 'What goals are you going to have in your programme if you can't measure? If you are trying to increase the immigrants you recruit, or improve those in managerial grades, sooner or later you have to measure something.'[14] The dilemma is summed up by Favell:

> There is a profound moral truth in the French refusal to actually recognize any French citizen of non-national 'ethnic' origin as such in official statistics, because the recognition itself can indeed be a form of inequality or discrimination. … Yet, on the other hand, no policy can be devised for systematic integration of foreign-origin groups until the nation-state begins to collectively recognize and classify minorities of ethnic origin, with special claims – targeted policies, resources, legal allowances, etc. – that follow from this (Favell 2003: 29)

There is great variety within the EU in the degree to which a member state's census or national population register is useful for identifying racial/ethnic inequality, or for operating and judging the effectiveness of anti-discrimination activities. In the UK ethnic monitoring within organisations is often used to evaluate the progress of policies, and these organisational statistics can be compared and related to, for example, national statistics on the ethnic breakdown of the locality. This is possible in the UK because a question on ethnic background has formed part of the official census since 1991. In Ireland, a similar question was added to the census for the first

---

14 Personal interview March 2001.

time in 2006. However, in this, the UK and Ireland form an EU minority. In some other countries their official population data registers whether the individual's parents were born abroad, making thus possible the identification of second generation immigrants, but no more than this. In most of the 10 new member states which joined the EU in 2004 there is a question on 'nationality' which is understood more in ethnic terms than in terms of citizenship, and can be used to identify members of long-standing national minorities within a country's borders (for example, Hungarians in Slovakia). However, these are incapable identifying more recent immigrant groups. Most of the remaining countries ask only about citizenship and place of birth. This means that in most EU countries official data is of limited use for the purpose of identifying groups subject to racial/ethnic discrimination, and evaluating measures against it (see Makkonen 2007).

Further national differences

Clearly, there are wide variations within Europe with regard to the acceptability of some important components of diversity management or equal opportunity practice, at levels 5 and 6. There may also be national differences in the acceptability of activities at other levels. Levels 4 and 3 in turn emphasise tackling everyday discrimination and racism. The concept of racism itself can be expressed differently between European countries, and this can have corresponding implications for the character of measures to counter racism and discrimination. We can illustrate this by contrasting again the cases of the United Kingdom and France. It is suggested by Michael Banton that policies in France start with the assumption that the causes of racism lie within the realm of ideas, and that the first priority is therefore to penalise incitement to racial hatred. Official discourses on racism are concerned with phenomena such as racial attacks, attack on mosques or Jewish cemeteries, or the incitement to racial hatred. Correspondingly, the policing of the press and publications regarding racism is much stricter than it is in Britain. In Britain, official policy makes no similar usage of the concept of racism but emphasises action against discriminatory behaviour in a rather pragmatic approach (Banton 1996). Thus it may be the case that level 3 anti-racist activities find a more sympathetic context in France than level 4, whereas in the UK people may be happier with a level 4 pragmatic anti-discrimination approach.

It might be predicted that level 2 – making cultural and religious allowances – is relatively uncontroversial, and that examples would be found easily in most member states. Evidence submitted to the EUMC in the 2000s suggests a growing willingness to make allowances for cultural and religious differences in European companies. For example, in Belgium, in March 2005, the Centre for Equal Opportunities and Opposition to Racism presented a report on 'Active public expressions of religious and philosophical convictions', based on surveys in organisations in both in the public and private sector, suggesting that employers generally saw little problem in making such allowances (CEOOR 2005). In Germany some of the larger international companies come to agreements with Muslim employees regarding religious holidays, enabling them to take those days off or can take unpaid leave.[15] In Ford (Cologne) special spaces for prayer have been set up for Muslims in order to enable them to pray at the workplace, attention is paid to the special needs of Muslims concerning the food that is offered in their canteens, and the canteens remain open after sunset during the time of Ramadan (Cözmez 2002).

Nevertheless, there are some countries where the practical recognition of ethnic minority culture and religion in the workplace may be problematic. For example, in Denmark, according to an NGO working for the better labour market integration of immigrants, in the early 2000s it was extremely difficult to find even basic examples of multicultural allowances, such as allowing Muslim women employees to wear the headscarf or *hijab*, or allowing Muslim workers to take Muslim rather than Christian religious holidays. Although by the middle of the 2000s some of the larger Danish companies were providing rooms in which Muslim workers could pray, the situation was still described in 2005 as one of 'massive discrimination in Denmark in the religious area' with most companies considering themselves to be 'religion-neutral zones' (Zarrehparvar and Hildebrandt 2005: 65). The wearing of the *hijab* remained a controversial issue, and in 2005 the Supreme Court of Denmark decided that the dismissal of an employee of a supermarket for having worn a headscarf for religious reasons in disregard of company clothing rules did not amount to indirect discrimination because the clothing rules were 'objectively justified'.[16]

Making active allowance for cultural diversity is a standard component of diversity management policies, indicating that such diversity is positively valued. Similarly, in a diversity policy the linguistic variety associated with workers of different cultural backgrounds is seen as something positive for the organisation. Yet in Denmark in 2006 it was reported that several major Danish companies, including a bus company and supermarket chain, had forbidden their employees to use any language other than Danish when dealing with customers, even when the clients come from the same ethnic minority origin as the person on the check-out, or as the person driving the bus.[17] Such a regulation represents the complete opposite of a diversity management approach, where the ability of staff to serve customers in their own language is regarded as an asset to the organisation.

Policies on the wearing of symbols of religious faith

There is great national variety within Europe regarding the right of employees to wear the headscarf at work. In the UK, this is generally not defined as a 'problem' or seen to be a public issue. This contrasts with Germany, for example, where each state or 'Land' has the right to pass a law prohibiting the display of religious symbols by state officials in public service, including teachers. Thus legislation banning the wearing of headscarves by teachers has been introduced in Saarland, Baden Wurttemberg

---

15 DGB Bildungswerk/Migration und Qualifikation, chapter 4.3.1.

16 Supreme Court UfR 2005.1265H.

17 Metroxpress 4. January 2006.

and Lower Saxony.[18] However, in Saarland and Lower Saxony Christian and Jewish symbols are excluded from the bans. Similarly, in 2005 a draft law by the Hessian state parliament would ban headscarves in civil service employment which again would not apply to Christian and Jewish symbols in the context of the 'Christian and Humanist influenced occidental tradition' of the State of Hesse (EUMC 2005).

Among EU member states there is also wide variety in approaches to the display of religious symbols in the education sphere (EUMC 2005, 2006a). Legislation prohibiting the wearing of headscarves or other identifiers of religious faith by pupils in schools have been or are being introduced in a number of member states, most notably in France, where the law on the application of the principle of secularity in schools was adopted in March 2004.[19] This bans the wearing of signs or clothes ostensibly manifesting religious beliefs of any kind. Whilst policies regarding pupils in schools are not directly the concern of diversity management policies in employment, it has been reported by French Muslims that the ban in schools was a signal for a more general resistance to the wearing of headscarves in employment (EUMC 2006b).

Such national differences in policies seem to be reflected in public opinion. In a public opinion survey in 17 countries in 2005, in answer to a question on whether there should be a ban on the wearing of headscarves by Muslim women in public places including schools, 78 percent of respondents in France and 54 per cent in Germany saw this as a 'good idea', compared to only 29 per cent in Great Britain.[20]

Citizenship and legal status

One important factor which will have direct implications for the acceptability and relevance of diversity management in an EU country is the legal status of ethnic minority workforce within it. The working population of the EU can be divided into five main categories in terms of legal status (Wrench 1996: 3).

1. Citizens living and working within their own country of citizenship. This includes people of immigrant origin who have become naturalised.
2. Citizens of an EU Member State who work in another country within the Union (EU denizens).
3. Third country nationals who have full rights to residency and work in a Member State (non-EU denizens).
4. Third country nationals whose employment in the country is constrained by a revocable work or residence permit, often for a fixed period of time. (This could include refugees who have been given permission to work.)
5. Undocumented or 'illegal' workers. (This may include asylum seekers whose application for refugee status is pending, or has been rejected.)

---

18 At the time of writing it was reported that a similar law was being planned by the state parliament in Bavaria.

19 Law no. 2004–228 of 15 March 2004 (JORF no. 65 du 17 mars 2004 page 5190).

20 Pew Global Attitudes Project: Islamic Extremism – Common Concern for Muslim and Western Publics, 14. 07.05.

The above five categories reflect formal status, and a continuum of rights ranging from full rights and privileges of citizenship in group 1 to the least rights of all in group 5. It is clear that the relevance of a diversity management approach in any particular country will differ according to which categories most of its migrant and minority ethnic workers fall in to. It will be most relevant to EU countries where migrants and ethnic minorities are skewed towards the top groups of the five legal categories of worker. Here, the immigrant population is likely to be longer established and issues of the 'second generation' are important, with concern over the unjustified exclusion of young people of migrant descent from employment opportunities by informal discrimination on 'racial' or ethnic grounds, and their over-representation in unemployment. In countries where most migrants and their descendants are found in category 1, legal discrimination in employment against non-citizens does not constitute a major problem, and a major part of anti-discrimination activity concerns tackling the informal discrimination which in practice reduces the opportunities of minority ethnic workers. Many components of an equal opportunities or diversity management policy aim to address such informal discrimination.

In some European countries, a high proportion of ethnic minority workers fall into category 3, suffering not only informal racial discrimination but also some formal legal discrimination. The labour market rights of non-EU denizens vary considerably between different European countries. For example, in some countries, nationals of non-EU countries, even when legally permanently resident and lawfully employed within the country, are excluded from a whole range of jobs, usually in the public sector, and may be entitled only to lower levels of unemployment benefit. In countries of southern Europe immigrants are more likely to be over-represented towards the bottom of the five groups, and the legal differences between the immigrant population and the national majority are even greater. Category 4 workers are often actively preferred and recruited because they are more vulnerable and less able to resist exploitation in terms of work intensity or working hours. In conditions where legal discrimination exists, a diversity management approach would seem to be premature.

Examples with regard to category 4 would be Slovenia and Austria. In Slovenia access to the labour market for third country nationals is regulated by a restrictive quota policy, directing non-nationals into the jobs with lower wages and poorer working conditions that are avoided by nationals, and allowing them only temporary contracts. Austria has retained a 'guestworker' approach with regard to its immigrants, who remain on a range of different work and residence permits. Although this has not kept immigrants from settling, it leaves the right to end their residence in the hands of the authorities, and constrains their working lives with restrictions not applicable to Austrian workers. Legal restrictions on immigrants ensure that large sections of immigrant workers remain complementary to native workers, and do not endanger their employment prospects (Gächter 2000). Even immigrants with a so-called 'permanent' work permit risk losing it if they have a period of unemployment, and become treated as new immigrants again. This keeps immigrant workers in a much weaker position than their Austrian co-workers. This weakness was compounded by the fact that until 2006 foreign workers were not able to be elected to be a member of a works council (Gächter 1997). This left whole sections of employment where immigrants were concentrated without proper representation at work. In such circumstances, anti-discrimination practice or diversity will take on a very different form to one in a country where such restrictions do not apply.

For example, one of the Austrian case studies for the European Compendium of Good Practice (see Chapter 3) described the only instance in the private sector in Austria where in the 1990s a deliberate attempt was made to circumvent this legal discrimination with regard to works councils. The case was a textile company where it had been the tradition for each department to be represented on the works council, and where, in the finishing department, where less than 10 per cent of the 67 staff were Austrian nationals, it was not possible to find a candidate. Through a creative exploitation of a loophole in the law, the company managed to get a Kurdish man on to the works council. The company then signed a separate agreement which stated that this man was to be treated as if he had the same rights and duties as a regularly elected works council member. One of the contextual factors in this case was that the head of personnel had recently joined the company from Germany, where the right for foreigners to be elected to works councils had existed since 1972, and so for him the idea did not seem at all unusual or threatening. 'At most he regarded the ban itself, and the elaborate route to circumvent it, as somewhat bizarre. His attitude undoubtedly helped the whole project' (Gächter 1997). This case illustrates how fighting discrimination, is, in the context of workers in the bottom groups of categories, just as likely to be fighting legal discrimination as the more conventionally understood organisational measures against racial discrimination. Given the continuing and dominating effect of legal restrictions on immigrant workers in Austria, it is perhaps not surprising that a telephone survey conducted in July 2005 among Austrian top managers working for companies with more than 250 employees showed that diversity management was 'not at all on the corporate agenda' in Austria.[21]

In countries where a major proportion of immigrants are found in category 5 – undocumented workers – then diversity management is even less appropriate as an anti-discrimination measure. To talk about 'ethnic monitoring', 'positive action' or 'valuing diversity' in an environment where immigrants are legally constrained into taking jobs others don't want, in worse conditions and at lower pay, or where large numbers of undocumented workers suffer intense exploitation, would be entirely inappropriate. One of the Spanish case studies originally submitted to the European Compendium of Good Practice (Cachón 1997) exemplifies how 'preventing discrimination' in the context of the widespread use of undocumented labour can be very different from elsewhere. This was a small agricultural enterprise in Saragossa, a province in the Aragón region of Spain. In this area, the fruit and vegetable farms which have developed on irrigated land employ large numbers of immigrant workers, since local agricultural workers have moved to other sectors to find better pay and conditions. The case study was an enterprise growing tomatoes, melons, onions and cereals, using immigrants for the labour intensive work. The owners operated according to a number of principles, many of which enable them to be seen in the Spanish context as 'good practice' against discrimination. The enterprise

---

21 *Der Standard*, (07./08.01.2006),'Human Resources sind Zukunftsthema', p. D2.

always hires legal immigrants, although they have frequently been approached for work by undocumented immigrants, and the employers take responsibility for all the immigrants' administrative formalities with the Provincial Employment Office. They hire immigrants of the same nationality (Moroccans), who are always men, aged between 20 and 40, and these are recruited through the networks of friends and relatives of existing workers. When one of their workers has a relative still living in Morocco who wishes to come to work there, they assist with the provision of relevant documents. The pay, contract of employment and working conditions of the Moroccans are always the same as those of the Spanish workers employed by the same enterprise. The enterprise provides accommodation for its workers, including a purpose built house which can accommodate 25 workers. Finally, the owners make allowances for the Moroccan workers culture – they assume that output will fall during Ramadan, and allow workers to return home for important feast times in the calendar.

Viewed from outside Spain, this enterprise may not look like an exemplary case of 'good practice' against racism and discrimination, and some of its practices are the complete antithesis of good diversity management. However, this case study has to be seen in the context of the fact that a large proportion of agricultural workers in Spain are undocumented, living and working in appalling conditions (Cachón 1999), and that this factor itself can foster racism. This is demonstrated by the incident which happened in February 2000, when the worst outbreak of racist violence in Spain's recent history occurred in El Ejido, a small Andalusian town of about 50,000 people and 15,000 immigrants from Morocco and Algeria working in the agricultural sector. Three days of violence and arson against immigrants and their houses, cars, shops and mosques, sparked off by the murder of a Spanish national, left 56 people requiring medical attention. Many of the immigrants worked illegally, grossly exploited for poor wages and living in appalling conditions. A trade union spokesman stated 'They are working and living in nineteenth century conditions. It is terrible. They live in caves, tents – they have no drinking water, electricity or hot water. Employers like them because they can pay low wages below the agreed levels. They are often single men and nothing has been done to foster their integration in the locality' (Wrench 2004: 79). The racist incidents were seen to be directly related to the employment of 'illegal' workers – as one commentator put it 'the demand for cheap manual labour generates the vicious circle of illegal immigration, underground employment, segregation and racism (....) Co-existence with people that live and work in subhuman conditions is obviously not easy'.[22]

Migrant workers such as agricultural workers in Spain on temporary contracts are segregated from Spanish workers, doing unpleasant jobs that the locals don't want to do. The areas where large numbers of immigrants work on temporary contracts were traditionally untouched by equal employment opportunity or conventional anti-discrimination policies, and in such circumstances diversity management policies are similarly irrelevant. However, the continuance or extension of a 'gastarbeiter mentality' into higher status jobs in the normal labour marker does have implications for diversity management. For example, in 2000 there was a German initiative –

---

22 *Eiro*nline, www.eiro.eurofound.ie, April 2000.

dubbed Germany's 'green card' scheme – which aimed to alleviate its information technology shortages by inviting computer experts from countries such as India to live and work in Germany for up to five years. This, according to one commentator was 'helping to sustain the old myth that one day, if circumstances change, the foreigners may all go and leave Germany to the Germans. The green card holders are ultimately modern, hi-tech guestworkers' (*Guardian* 31 October 2000). [23] This kind of policy does not sit well with the sort of organisational culture which is supposed to be fostered by diversity management – a heterogeneous pluralistic culture where all differences are valued – when sections of ethnically – or nationally-differentiated workers are marked out in a legally inferior position to their colleagues.

National myths and political discourse

Whilst the above differences are related to clearly differentiated legal variations in status, there are equally significant variables of national ideology, culture and politics which are relevant to the dissemination of diversity management.

There are important differences in 'national myths' which have implications for the acceptability of policies relating to immigrants and ethnic minorities. In countries such as the USA, Canada and Australia, which have been built on immigrants, the idea of immigration has been a relatively positive theme in national development. European countries, on the other hand, see their cohesion as coming from nationality or ethnicity rather than the 'strength through diversity' which is associated with traditional immigration countries. (It has been noted by others that someone in the US who would be called a 'second-generation American' would be called in most European countries a 'second-generation immigrant'.) The different views of the nation are summed up by Favell as follows:

> In Europe we are talking about tightly bounded and culturally specific nation-states dealing in the post-war period with an unexpected – but still not very large – influx of highly diverse immigrant settlers, at a time when, for other international reasons, their sense of nationhood is insecure or in decline. It is a problematic very different to those faced by the US or Australia, whose histories and sense of nationhood have always been built on immigration. Europe, rather, faces a problematic where the continuity of nation-building is perhaps a much more significant fact than the multicultural hybridity that is sometimes sought for in these other, newer 'model' nations (Favell 2003: 30).

One difference between the European and the US context is that in America there is an assumption that immigrant populations will eventually become full and equal members of society, and that their children born on American soil will become American citizens. This is not so in some European countries where the acquisition of citizenship is made difficult for immigrants of long-term residence, and even for their children born in that country.

---

23 In 2001, after the scheme generated far less recruits than was hoped, a government appointed commission recommended that a proportion (20,000 workers a year) of those highly skilled workers required should be given permanent right of abode in Germany (*Guardian* 5 July 2001).

There are also great differences, historically and culturally, *within* Europe in national responses to immigration and ethnic diversity. Castles (1995) provides an 'ideal type' categorisation of such responses, which includes *differential exclusion* – immigrants are seen as guest workers without full social and political rights, *assimilation* – immigrants are awarded full rights but are expected to become like everyone else, and *pluralism/multi-culturalism* – immigrants have full rights but maintain some cultural differences.

The implications of Castles' model will be explored next, drawing on modifications by Kirton and Greene (2000), and extra material from Bryant (1997), and Wren and Boyle (2002). First, the categories need further explanation.

Differential exclusion

Immigrants are seen as guest workers (gastarbeiters) without full social and political rights. Citizenship is defined by descent. Naturalisation is possible for non-nationals but requires the renunciation of other citizenships and evidence of meeting the criteria for the national way of life and affiliation to the country. Civil society is suspicious of ethno-pluralism. Historically this categorises Germany, Austria, Switzerland and Belgium. In Germany, the guest worker approach fits into the idea of a German nation not as political entity confined by territorial boundaries, but as a 'Volk-centred ethnocultural' entity, where access to citizenship is based upon biological descent or *jus sanguinis* (see Heckmann 2003). This has allowed ethnic Germans who have never lived in Germany – for example those from Eastern Europe – access to citizenship rights more easily than second and third generation Turkish migrants born and educated in Germany. Until the end of the 20th century the ethnic nature of citizenship in Germany continued to be based on definitions of kinship and race as established by the Nuremberg Laws. Wren and Boyle in 2002 summarised the relationship of foreign workers with Germany as 'highly ambivalent', with liberal admission policies, and a relatively relaxed asylum policy, but denial of citizenship rights.

Assimilation

Immigrants are awarded full rights but are expected to assimilate to cultural norms. Unlike the differential exclusion model, citizenship is linked to a territorial community – the principle of *jus soli* – rather than based on descent. Dual nationality is not encouraged. This categorises France, and elements of this have been found in the UK in the 1960s. In contrast to the German model, the French state is conceived of as a largely political rather than a cultural entity, where political unity and not shared culture constitutes the nation. This allows 'others' to be incorporated with relative ease, and citizenship can be achieved through birth and residence. It is assumed that this assimilatory approach allows people to 'become French', and the universalist approach discourages the identification of ethnic origin in social policies.

Pluralism/multiculturalism

Immigrants have full rights but maintain some cultural differences. Dual nationality is allowed. Unlike the differential exclusion and assimilation models, different group identities are officially recognised. The accommodation of different ethnic cultures and norms is encouraged, although requiring a basic loyalty to the nation. This has categorised the Netherlands and Sweden. In the Netherlands, for example, a pluralistic approach allowed the development of separate institutions, such as schools, trade unions and political parties, for people of different religions. Thus the concept of minority groups was relatively easy to incorporate into Dutch society due to this pre-existing 'pillarisation', or 'living-apart-together' framework. (Wren and Boyle 2002). Policy in the Netherlands in the 1970s was encapsulated in the phrase 'the integration of ethnic minority groups while retaining the cultural identities of their countries of descent' (Glastra et al. 1998: 168). As in France, citizenship rights are based on principle of *jus soli,* and Dutch citizenship has been relatively easy to obtain. In Sweden citizenship is also relatively easily obtained. Immigrants were encouraged to settle permanently and become part of Swedish society, with the state promoting various integration policies in the context of an overall policy of multiculturalism. Westin (2000) shows how in the 1970s the 'traditional unreflected policy of assimilation' gave way to policies which entailed an acceptance that Sweden was turning into a multicultural society, facing a future of 'cultural pluralism' (Westin 2000: 20).

Kirton and Greene (2000: 237) classify Britain since the 1970s as 'pragmatist pluralism'. This is similar to the pluralist model but has come about in a *de facto* way rather than being legally defined. Immigrants have full rights and maintain some cultural differences, but this is in the context of a lack of a defined policy perspective. It is aided by the fact that '"British" has always been a composite identity, and is therefore easy to extend to other groups' (Bryant 1997). References to multiculturalism can be found in British political debate as far back as the mid 1960s, when a British Home Secretary referred to the integration of immigrants as implying the acceptance of 'cultural diversity' at the same time as 'equality of opportunity' in an atmosphere of 'mutual tolerance' (see Rex 2000: 202). In October 2000 an independent think tank produced a major report called 'The Future of Multi-Ethnic Britain', the aim being 'to propose ways of countering racial discrimination and disadvantage and making Britain a confident and vibrant multicultural society at ease with its rich diversity'. The report, which was launched by the British Home Secretary, recommended that Britain should develop both as a community of citizens and as a 'community of communities' (the pluralist view) (Parekh et al. 2000). And in 2001 the British Foreign Secretary made a speech stating that the British are not a 'race' and Britishness cannot be defined in terms of race or ethnic background. The speech was described in one newspaper as 'one of the strongest defences of multiculturalism made by a Government minister' (*Guardian* 19 April 2001). The general acceptance of multiculturalism in British public opinion is reflected in a survey in the UK conducted by MORI in August 2005, (one month after the 7th July bombings in London by Islamic extremists), where 62 per cent of respondents agreed that 'multiculturalism makes Britain a better place to live' (Jedwab 2005: 95).

The word 'multiculturalism' can be used in different ways. It may be used just to describe a demographic condition whereby a country is 'multicultural' just by the presence of people whose origins are elsewhere. More usefully, it is used to describe a condition in opposition to 'assimilation' so that immigrants are not expected to discard all their own values and practices and become like the majority. The term is associated with mutual tolerance, and rights to preserve aspects of cultural heritage and language, to maintain religious and cultural institutions, and to engage in religious and cultural practices, in the context of equal treatment and equality before the law (see Vertovec and Wessendorf 2005).

The relevance for diversity management

The question for this book is whether we should expect to find certain important elements of organisational anti-discrimination policies, such as positive action and 'celebrating diversity', only in the context of the third category, pluralism/multiculturalism, as they would not seem to sit naturally in the context of a dominant 'assimilationist' or 'gastarbeiter' approach. Certainly this might be expected to be the case if reality reflected exactly these categories within each country. However, these are 'ideal' types, and in reality there has been some tensions within them and some practical leeway. For example, Castles states that the *differential exclusion* model was based on the desire to prevent permanent settlement, and has proved hard to maintain because it leads to social tension and contradicts the democratic principle of including all members of civil society in the nation-state. In Germany there has been something of a shift from this model to assimilation policies in some areas, and some multi-cultural policies in education. In 2001 the government-appointed Süssmuth commission called on Germans to abandon the 'fiction' that Germany is not a country of immigration (*Guardian* 5 July 2001). The new German immigration reforms, adopted by the German parliament in March 2002, cover new measures for actively recruiting immigrants, and for the first time define Germany as an immigrant-receiving country. In this, Germany is moving away from the old 'guestworker' model towards a more 'universalistic' model. (Probably Austria has remained as a purer type of this model than Germany – Gächter 2000.)

In France, probably the best example of the *assimilation* model with its republican tradition of 'equal treatment for all', there has been a move to some elements of the pluralist model. Also in France in 1993 there was a move towards in the other direction towards a harder *gastarbeiter* model when the Pasqua laws reversed measures which previously allowed migrant workers to renew their permits at regular intervals and allowed citizenship after a certain period of years, thus rendering illegal thousands of previously legal migrant workers (Kirton and Greene 2000: 238). In the Netherlands there has been some serious government retrenchment from earlier multicultural positions, culminating in a much-criticised integration bill proposed in 2005, and in Britain in 2006 there were moves by political leaders questioning pluralist conceptions of society and introducing the discourse of assimilation and 'core values'.

Thus there are inconsistencies and counter-tendencies in those European countries which fit close to the 'ideal types'. Nevertheless, imperfectly though the 'multicultural' ideologies are expressed in practice, the countries where they are expressed have provided a more sympathetic context for organisational equity policies for immigrants and ethnic minorities than a country such Germany, where the official line was maintained for 20 years or more, against all the evidence, that 'Germany is not a country of immigration', or Denmark, where much public discourse remains assimilationist. Although there are contradictory examples in practices, the ideologies relating to the 'ideal types' set out by Castles often remain in public discourse, and are directly reflected in how policies on the treatment of migrants and ethnic minorities are expressed. As Schnapper et al. (2003: 15) state: 'Ideologies have an effect on reality. They are transformed into legal and institutional measures which influence everyday life and are internalised by the population.' The contrasting associated national 'myths' in Europe do provide very different contexts in which organisational policies are located.

Political impediments to diversity management

Related to the above, it seems that in some European countries the national political discourse does not provide a particularly sympathetic environment for the adoption of diversity management policies by employers. Indeed we can go so far as to say that in some circumstances it may militate directly against it. An example of the latter is Denmark. In recent years, cultural racism has become a normal part of Danish political and media discourse, in the context of an unthinking assimilationism (Schierup 1993). 'Public racist slurs have become commonplace (and legally tolerated), and political parties across the spectrum have adopted cultural racism as an integral part of their platforms' (Wren 2001: 146). Right wing politicians in Denmark play on public fears that foreigners will flood into the country and take advantage of the Danish social welfare system. Mainstream political discourse on the subject of immigrants and refugees has shifted markedly to the right in recent years, and the views of right-wing politicians which were once considered extreme or racist are now uttered by 'respectable' people in mainstream organisations. In 2000 the (Social Democratic) Minister of the Interior felt the need to forcefully reassure the public that 'Denmark will never be a multicultural society'. The 2005 report on Denmark by the European Commission against Racism and Intolerance (ECRI) concluded with regard to the climate of opinion in Denmark that 'there is a pervasive atmosphere of intolerance and xenophobia against refugees, asylum seekers, as well as minority groups in general and Muslims in particular. The media, together with politicians play a major role in creating this atmosphere' (ECRI 2006: 29).

According to some practitioners, the general climate of discourse from the government, politicians and the media has had a direct negative impact on the development of diversity management. One consequence of this is that in Denmark the private labour market has been ahead of the public one on diversity issues. As mentioned earlier, an organisation called 'Foreningen Nydansker' was set up in June 1998 by a number of large businesses with the aim of influencing public debate and setting a 'positive agenda' in the business community regarding the employment of 'new Danes'. However, activists in this organisation reported that they were 'swimming against the tide' when trying to promote more broadly a diversity management consciousness. One reported that when he meets with employers to discuss with them the possibility of adopting diversity management policies the employers reply that the government has pronounced that Denmark is not a multicultural society, and that 'government integration polices will make Danish people out of the immigrants'. Therefore, say the employers, 'why do we need to introduce policies which make allowances for cultural differences when in five years there won't be any?' He also reported that those employers who might be sympathetic to taking on more immigrant employees were concerned about customer reaction, and concluded 'As long as the politicians won't put any demands on the Danes, then companies can't put any demands on the customers'.[24]

Thus we can see some of the implications of the variety of contexts which exist in Europe. Sometimes employers and their organisations have been historically resistant to the very idea of organisational anti-discrimination policies, in some contexts the notion that such policies can be constructed using the dimension of ethnic origin goes against the grain of public debate, sometimes political leaders take the initiative in pressing employers to adopt diversity policies, whilst elsewhere politicians actively hinder the desires of employers to adopt them.

Trade unions and diversity management

It is not only the variety in attitudes and actions of employers and politicians which is relevant to the spread of diversity management, but also trade unions and employees. According to the European Commission's questionnaire survey on good practice in workplace diversity, referred to earlier in this chapter (European Commission 2005), many of the 'good practice' companies identified support from trade unions, works councils and other staff groups and networks as a prerequisite for the successful implementation of diversity policies. One criticism made of American models of diversity management has been that they have focused too strongly on management action and neglected trade union influences (Berg and Håpnes 2001). Whilst a strong commitment by senior management is an essential element – almost a defining feature – of diversity management, an *over*-strong emphasis on management reflects the US situation of relatively low levels of unionisation. In Scandinavian countries, by contrast, unionisation is very high, and there is a tradition of consultation and agreement between employers and unions on issues of major significance to the organisation. In their study of diversity practices in Norwegian companies, Berg and Håpnes show that in private sector companies a close collaboration between management and employees was considered to be very important for the success of integration processes for ethnic minority employees. Similarly in Denmark, unionisation lies somewhere between 80–90 per cent, in the context of a strong tradition of collective bargaining. Employers who do not observe agreements,

---

24 Personal interview September 2001.

for example, on pay, can be held to account and this has been a major source of union power (Scheuer 1992). The trade union monopoly in representing employee interests in the labour courts has also been a major advantage in attracting members (Lind 1995), as is the link between being a member of a union and membership of an unemployment insurance system. Thus in Denmark and other Scandinavian countries it is hard to imagine the development of diversity management policies in organisations without union participation.

At first sight it would seem that trade unions in Europe would on principle support diversity management and its principles of sensitivity to cultural diversity amongst their members. For example, in 2005 in Belgium the Flemish divisions of the national trade unions – the ACV, ABVV and ACLVB – initiated a project in the framework of the European EQUAL anti-discrimination programme to sensitise activists and union representatives on issues of diversity and non-discrimination on the shop floor.[25] However, just as employers' groups and politicians across Europe can vary in their receptiveness to diversity policies, so can trade unions. Historically there have been very different national responses by European trade unions to immigrants and ethnic minorities in their respective countries (Penninx and Roosblad 2000). Is it possible that some trade unions will be unsympathetic to notions of cultural diversity on principle? In France during 1990s the right wing anti-immigrant *Front National* managed to take over local union control in some parts of the country, and in Italy, in October 2000, the trade union connected to the *Lega Nord*, a similarly right wing and anti-immigrant political party, for the first time gained more votes than other unions in the elections for worker representatives in a major company (the Michelin plant in Piedmont). Trade unions associated with right wing political parties are likely to have little time for the concept of diversity management. Yet it is not only from the Right that unions can oppose diversity management. In 1997 a motion was passed at the Black Workers Conference of the UK Trades Union Congress (TUC) opposing the trend towards diversity management in British companies (see Chapter 5). In order to illustrate how national trade union movements can exhibit contrasting attitudes to diversity management we can turn to one comparison of trade unions in Europe, namely the UK and Denmark.

Danish and British trade union responses to diversity management

This comparison highlighted the very different responses to diversity management exhibited by trade union ethnic equality activists in the UK and Denmark (Wrench 2004; Greene et al. 2005). Interviews revealed that in Denmark diversity management tended to be looked upon favourably, whereas in Britain it was regarded with great suspicion. Consistent with the opposition to diversity management expressed at the 1997 TUC national Black Workers' Conference, the interviews with the British trade union activists revealed attitudes ranging from scepticism to outright hostility to diversity management. Respondents saw it as a managerial strategy which took the anti-discrimination initiative away from trade unions, did nothing to challenge the

---

25 http://www.colourfulworkshop.be.

basis of racial discrimination, and simply emphasised cultural diversity as a way of improving service delivery. The scepticism of the British trade unionists interviewed by Wrench (2004) was confirmed by Greene and Kirton (2003) who during the same period interviewed British trade union officials holding responsibility for equalities issues and also discovered a great deal of suspicion about the managing diversity rhetoric. The officials perceived 'diversity' to be purely a 'managerialist' intervention whereas 'equality' issues were more in the hands of the trade unions. One saw it as 'a cover-up or not really doing anything' and another described it as a 'softer term' which detracted from the equality agenda. A third felt that 'diversity is very easy as a window dressing and it's very convenient for management if you don't really want to do anything' (Greene and Kirton 2003: 9–10).

In the Danish interviews there was no evidence of any such suspicion. All those who were aware of diversity management were strongly in favour of it, and saw it as the way forward in Denmark. For example, the white collar union with the strongest ethnic equality policy in Denmark was planning to convert its ethnic equality programme into a broader diversity policy. A respondent employed at one of the main institutes in Denmark responsible for providing training courses for trade unions was planning training on topics such as 'intercultural communication', 'diversity management' and 'the diverse working place', and emphasised 'I want to establish the foundation of diversity in everything we do here'.

Differing experiences of equality policies

There seemed to be several factors which accounted for this difference in attitudes of trade union activists. Firstly, in Britain, unlike in Denmark, there has been a long history of ethnic equality and anti-discrimination measures in UK unions, with some bitter struggles having been necessary before getting to a stage where reasonably strong equal opportunities, anti-racist and anti-discrimination policies started to become accepted, both in the workplace and within the unions themselves (Wrench 1987). In the light of this experience, British equal opportunities activists seemed to be suspicious that diversity management might be a backwards step, used to selectively prioritise 'soft' rather than 'hard' equal opportunities practices, and avoiding positive action measures, for example. (For more detail on this and other criticisms of diversity management see Chapter 5.)

In contrast, the Danish trade unions have had no comparable experience of long-established equal opportunities or anti-discrimination policies. However, they have, in recent years, become increasingly conscious of the problem of ethnic discrimination in the labour market (for example, see Hjarnø and Jensen 1997; Møller and Togeby 1999) and the need to respond in some way. Not having had the same experience as British unions, they do not see diversity management as an alternative to, or something that will undermine, their previous efforts. Instead, Danish ethnic equality activists are more likely to see diversity management as a timely and positive development to get ethnic equality practices onto the agenda and help to break down the barriers to equal employment that exist within the Danish labour market.

Contrasting industrial relations traditions

A second relevant factor is the different industrial relations traditions in the two countries. In Denmark industrial relations is characterised by greater cooperation and interdependence between the two sides, whereas in Britain conflict and confrontation are seen as more 'normal'. The characteristics of Danish industrial relations have been summed up as 'a highly organised labour market both on the employers' and the employees' sides, with widespread co-operation and consensus between trade unions and employers and their organisations' (Lind 2000: 146). In contrast, British unions have not had the political legitimacy and institutionalised cooperation of their Danish counterparts, and their overall stance has been characterised historically as 'a resistance to change and an adversarial posture in the workplace' (Edwards et al 1992: 5).

It seems that diversity management fits well into the 'consensus' way of doing things characteristic of Danish industrial relations, with an emphasis on consultation with management as a way of addressing problems such as racial inequality, in contrast with the more combative approach of fighting racism characteristic of British unions. Unlike in the UK, Danish unions are used to co-operating with employers far more, and many large Danish employers themselves also welcome the development of diversity management.

Different contexts of multiculturalism

A third contextual factor which is important in understanding the difference in receptivity to diversity management between the two countries is the way that the concept of multiculturalism features in national discourse. As stated earlier, in Britain, political leaders will intermittently endorse this concept; in Denmark, not only is there no official political endorsement of multiculturalism, but it is more likely to be actively and vehemently opposed. If we return to Castles three major categorisations of national differences in responses to immigration and ethnic diversity – the guestworker approach, assimilationism and multiculturalism (Castles 1995) – then we can classify the dominant approaches in the UK and Denmark respectively as multicultural and assimilationist. However, there is no reason to assume that the labour movements in each country will automatically agree with the dominant national discourse. For example, the trade union movement in Germany abandoned the 'gastarbeiter' view of immigration long before the German government did, and similarly did not embrace the government's fiction that 'Germany is not a country of immigration' (Kühne 2000). In Denmark, the labour movement activists' opposition to the government's assimilationist discourse has been expressed in a general *support* for the ideas of multiculturalism, and this is also consistent with a generally positive view towards the introduction of diversity management by union leaders. In the context of the extremely negative Danish political discourse on multiculturalism, the promotion of diversity management is seen to be a positive development by ethnic minority and trade union activists as well as by many leading employers. Furthermore, multiculturalism sits very well with a diversity management approach which celebrates the business benefits of a culturally diverse workforce. In Denmark, the embracing of a multicultural philosophy by unions is progressive in the context of a national debate where politicians generate an 'anti-multiculturalism' assimilationist discourse.

In contrast, in the UK, as stated earlier, a general 'multiculturalism' is relatively uncontroversial in comparison to some other EU countries, and for the union activists in Britain, a multicultural diversity management approach is contrasted not with 'anti-multiculturalism' in national discourse, but with an alternative ethnic equality approach, namely equal opportunities with elements of anti-discrimination and positive action. People who have been active in equality struggles within the British trade union movement see a move to diversity management as a retrograde, not progressive, step, in a context where there are already a great number of anti-racist, anti-discrimination and equal opportunities initiatives underway.

Therefore, in order to understand the differences in attitudes to diversity management between the union activists in the two countries we must be aware of these three sets of factors. Firstly, the different experiences of anti-discrimination activities prior to the entry of diversity management onto the scene pre-dispose them to exhibit very different responses to it. Secondly, it seems that the managing diversity approach favoured by the Danes and the combating inequality approach favoured by the British are respectively more consistent with the consensus and conflict dimensions of their industrial relations approaches. Thirdly, unlike in the UK, the dominant assimilationist, anti-immigrant and anti-multiculturalism discourse in Denmark by politicians and the media tends to produce a positive view of multicultural policies and the concept of diversity by trade union activists when they are opposing this discourse.

In conclusion, this comparison between just two EU countries can be used to make broader points regarding the development of diversity management, points which have been relatively neglected in the US literature. One is that European employers will need to recognise that the stances of trade unions are often going to be relevant and important considerations in their strategies for the adoption of diversity management. Another is to realise that trade union responses to diversity management may not be uniform across national boundaries, and that an understanding of this is aided by a sensitivity to the relevant historical, institutional, cultural and political differences of national context. The example of trade unions also indicates that opposition to diversity management can come from opposing ends of the political spectrum. In order to better understand how there can be resistance to diversity management from bodies representing both the Left and the Right, we need to explore in further detail some of the main critiques which have been made of diversity management over recent years. This will be done in the next chapter.

Chapter 5

An Overview of Critiques of Diversity Management

In the previous chapters there have been several references to specific criticisms of diversity management. At this stage it might be useful to further explore *critiques* of diversity management, as there now exists a body of critical literature on diversity management deriving from a wide spectrum of political and academic positions. This chapter will examine selected examples of these, each of which exemplifies a characteristic type of critique, and will use these to present a continuum of critiques, ranging from the minor to the fundamental. This exercise is useful in order to help us clarify critiques which come from widely different standpoints and interests. It also helps us to better understand the nature of types of diversity management.

The critiques are set out in order of the severity of their implications for diversity management. At the beginning are critiques which are not fundamental in their implications, and which are compatible with the continuing practice of diversity management. Some come from within a business paradigm, and aim to raise our understanding of diversity management, but without calling into question its continuing existence. One critique identifies diversity management as representing the sectional interest of one particular occupational group; others find that the benefits of diversity have been exaggerated, and that diversity in a workforce or workgroup should not be assumed to be beneficial in all circumstances. Finally, from a number of sources come criticisms of various practices that have taken place under the name of diversity management.

Then follow a group of critiques which ask more serious questions about the intrinsic nature of diversity management, particularly in comparison with earlier employment equity approaches. These come from people who are sympathetic to earlier equal opportunities or anti-discrimination approaches but who have particular criticisms of aspects which are intrinsic to the diversity management approach. Here, diversity management is seen as undermining previous approaches to combating racism and discrimination, such as legal measures or activities by trade unions. It is criticised for being a 'soft option', for diluting the racial and ethnic focus of equality activities, and for replacing a moral imperative by an economic one.

Finally, more radical critiques are introduced which question the basic premises of the whole diversity management approach, and which identify the development of this organisational practice as a negative or retrograde step. They might be classified as 'fundamental' or 'oppositional'. One accuses diversity management of perpetuating a major intellectual fallacy, namely, the reification of the concept of ethnicity. Other critiques in this section can be categorised as 'political', coming from both a Right and Left perspective. Whereas the former identify the ideology as a hangover from the misguided era of 'progressive' social engineering, the latter see it as neglecting structural determinants of inequality, and obscuring and mystifying inequalities of power. The apparently progressive aspects of diversity management are seen as a veneer which helps to maintain the status quo, and the ideology is seen as compatible with, and a reflection of, the new Right, economic liberalism and neo-conservative political forces.

Non-fundamental critiques

The first examples are critiques that demonstrate that we should not simply accept diversity management at face value, as portrayed in a standard human resource management textbook, but that we should look a little more critically at its origins, philosophy or claims. However, these are not fundamental or 'radical' critiques, because at the same time these arguments leave open the possibility that diversity management itself does have intrinsic merit and can be valuable for the organisation.

Diversity management as a sectional interest

The critique by Kelly and Dobbin (1998) portrays diversity management not simply as a neutral management practice adopted in response to the objective needs of a changing organisational world, but rather as something which has developed in order to serve the sectional interests of one particular occupational group. They trace the development of diversity management in the US in the 1980s in the context of the political assault on equal employment opportunities/affirmative action (EEO/AA). They outline four stages in American employers' response to AA and EEO law. First, in the 1960s, the ambiguity and weak enforcement of these laws led to few changes in employers' practices. Then, between 1972 and 1980, increased federal enforcement led employers to pay closer attention to anti-discrimination law, and during this period they started to hire EEO/AA specialists to devise strategies to comply with the law. In so doing, 'employers created internal constituencies that championed EEO/AA measures'.

The third stage was in the early 1980s when the Reagan administration began to criticise EEO/AA programmes and curtail enforcement. This was a time of 'backlash', with reverse-discrimination suits and state-level anti-affirmative action movements. However, despite this undermining of EEO/AA, many employers continued with the anti-discrimination practices that they already had in place, and EEO/AA specialists began to emphasise the efficiency gains that had followed the adoption of these earlier EEO/AA practices. Fourthly, after 1987, when the legal future of affirmative action remained uncertain and courts continued to 'chip away' at the law, EEO/AA specialists transformed themselves into diversity managers and promoted a range of human resource practices aimed at maintaining and managing diversity in the workforce (Kelly and Dobbin 1998: 963).

> In the 1980s and 1990s ... managerial and professional networks collectively constructed antidiscrimination practices as means to improving efficiency, at first by touting the gains

associated with formalizing hiring and promotion and later by touting the gains associated with using a diverse workforce to serve a diverse customer base. EEO/AA practices were soon recast as the diversity management component of the new human resources management paradigm. Practices designed to achieve legal compliance were retheorized as efficient when the original impetus for adopting them was removed (Kelly and Dobbin 1998: 962).

Kelly and Dobbin draw on the theoretical work of Selznick (1949, 1957) to show how an 'internal constituency' in the organisation – in this case, 'staff members whose positions, paychecks, and professional identities depended on the continuation of EEO and AA efforts' – managed to reinforce an organisational programme that seemed to have outlived its original purpose by re-theorising existing practices in new ways.

The next critiques are also 'non-fundamental', in that they are arguments from a perspective which does not reject diversity management in principle, but which criticise the fact that its claims are greatly exaggerated, or that in practice it may be carried out badly. These critiques ask for a more realistic approach to diversity management.

Diversity benefits overstated

One of the main claims of diversity management which has come under critical focus is the assumption that diversity automatically brings benefits to the organisation and workforce in terms of, for example, the increased productivity or creativity of diverse work groups. An American review of the literature (Williams and O'Reilly 1998) concluded that the 'diversity is good for organisations' mantra has been overstated. For example, they argue that most of the research which supports the claim that diversity is beneficial for groups has been conducted in a laboratory or classroom setting. Laboratory studies neglect the variable of time, and research in short-lived groups is not a strong foundation for judging the effects of diversity in a real organisation. The smaller number of studies which have looked at groups in an organisational context show a less optimistic view, with evidence of stereotyping and conflicts within groups. Some field studies have shown that race and gender diversity can have *negative* effects on group processes and performance (Williams and O'Reilly 1998: 80). After reviewing the literature, Williams and O'Reilly conclude that, under ideal conditions, increased diversity may have a positive impact through, for example, the increase in skill and knowledge that diversity brings. However, they argue that the preponderance of empirical evidence suggests that diversity is most likely to impede group functioning, and conclude:

> Unless steps are taken to actively counteract these effects, the evidence suggests that, by itself, diversity is more likely to have negative than positive effects on group performance. Simply having more diversity in a group is no guarantee that the group will make better decisions or function effectively. In our view, these conclusions suggest that diversity is a mixed blessing and requires careful and sustained attention to be a positive force in enhancing performance (Williams and O'Reilly 1998: 120).

Therefore, for Williams and O'Reilly, 'The challenge is to develop ways to accommodate these tendencies so that their negative effects are attenuated and the positive effects of diversity can be achieved' (Williams and O'Reilly 1998: 121).

Similarly, a later literature review by two American scholars (Wise and Tschirhart 2000) found that many of the promises and claims of diversity management for improving group and organisational performance could not be said to have been rooted in the findings of empirical research. They started their review from the position that 'empirical evidence about the consequences of diversity in work organizations is limited, and many of the existing studies present conflicting and inconclusive findings'. Wise and Tschirhart argue that managing-for-diversity practices cannot be informed by results of studies that link characteristics of people in an organisation with outcomes, without paying any attention to the interactions of these people and the causal connection of the interactions to the outcomes. For instance, they argue, members of different racial or ethnic groups may be found in the same organisation, but they may have little interaction as a consequence of occupational segregation or other factors – the overall diversity of the workforce has little relevance to task outcomes. To understand how to manage for diversity, 'we need studies that examine process and outcome consequences of the collective involvement of workers with perceived differences in a task setting and studies that explore the effects of different situational or contextual factors on organizational or group outcomes' (Wise and Tschirhart 2000: 387).

Wise and Tschirhart critically examined 106 empirical findings from 33 studies of the outcomes of diversity. For one thing, they found that the generalisabilty of many of the findings was limited due to the use of students as research subjects – 26 per cent of the studies did this. Generalisability was also compromised by the fact that in so many of the studies the interpersonal interaction that was studied was artificially constructed. They argue:

> Artificial scenarios … cannot duplicate … critical factors such as organizational size, structure, technology, and organizational communication mechanisms. In addition, artificial scenarios lack the historical, political, instrumental, and emotional contexts that real managing-for-diversity programs must address. The simulations have no real consequences for personal well-being and do not put at risk an individual's personal need fulfilment (Wise and Tschirhart 2000: 391).

Another important criticism of many studies is that some scholars and practitioners mistakenly believe that the results for one dimension of workplace diversity can be assumed to apply to other dimensions. For example, 'effects of sex diversity on performance ratings are not generalisable to racial diversity, yet many people have assumed that they are' (Wise and Tschirhart 2000: 39). Another weakness in the research literature affecting the utility of diversity research is the limited use of time-series studies. They argue that 'longitudinal research is especially important in the area of managing for diversity because the processes of mutual accommodation and integration that are considered critical to effective diversity management take time to develop.' There are only a handful of studies attempting to assess the consequences of diversity over time and these studies suggest that initial observations are quite different from those obtained at a later point. For example, they argue, 'homogeneous groups may appear in the initial observations to operate with less conflict or be more efficient at problem solving, but subsequent observations may show that there are no differences between homogeneous and heterogeneous groups'. Therefore, they conclude, if it is true that the consequences of diversity for small-group performance change over time, 'then research based on a single observation can be applied only to work groups sharing the same stage of development' (Wise and Tschirhart 2000: 392). In conclusion, Wise and Tschirhart summarise that 'Given the weaknesses in the body of research on diversity, we can draw no firm conclusions for public administrators. We cannot claim that diversity has any clear positive or negative effects on individual, group or organizational outcomes' (Wise and Tschirhart 2000: 392).

It should be recognised that Wise and Tschirhart deliberately restricted their enquiry to 'hypotheses testing' research published in scholarly journals, so as to maintain a minimum standard of quality in the research that they were reviewing. Their findings should not be taken to mean that there are no demonstrable benefits of a diverse workforce, or of managing for diversity. The evidence for this tends to be of another kind, namely the material within the case studies to be found in the diversity management literature. And as one Danish diversity management activist put it 'The fact that diversity management advantages are not scientifically proven should not worry us disproportionately – most human resource management is based on things that are not proven'.[1] The value of Wise and Tschirhart's work is to warn against the distortion and over-statement of academic research on diversity.

Diversity benefits overgeneralised

A criticism related to the previous one concerns the assumption that diversity in a workforce or work groups is beneficial for all organisations in all circumstances. Broomé, Carlson and Ohlsson (2000, 2001) introduce an 'input-transformation-output' model to demonstrate that the opportunities and risks of ethnic diversity for an organisation are not uniform. Thus the opportunities and risks of diversity for an organisation can be grouped by reference to three headings. The first is the *input* to the organisation, for example materials and personnel. Input questions for an organisation concern the utilisation of a larger potential workforce and a wider pool of talent to choose from. As a rule, they argue, this signifies increased opportunities for the organisation but hardly any risks. The risk that an individual organisation runs if it intends to remain ethnically homogeneous is of selecting from a smaller supply of labour or a smaller pool of talent. Broomé et al. state 'For the majority of organisations, which of course are small, such a risk must be regarded as relatively little, as the net labour market supply changes slowly and a sufficient labour supply exists from the majority population.' However, they argue, for large organisations, or for entire branches or sectors of the economy, the analysis works out quite differently. (This may be one of the reasons why it tends to be the larger organisations which more readily embrace diversity management.)

---

1   Personal interview September 2001.

The second heading is the organisation's *internal* functions, for example the division of labour, technology and management. In this case, there are clearly both opportunities and risks of diversity which can influence the internal life of the organisation and its way of functioning and working. On the one hand there might be increased flexibility, creativity, employee loyalty, openness, criticism and knowledge transference; on the other, there might be communication problems, ethnocentrism, ethnic conflicts, stereotyping, culture clash, or reduced trust and openness.

Broomé et al. argue that it is important to differentiate which firms or parts of a firm have need for increased creativity, increased critical scrutiny, increased flexibility, increased knowledge transference and other possible effects of ethnic diversity of the workforce. For example, least sensitive to ethnic diversity is the production of goods, where there is likely to be a high degree of uniformity of production. Therefore 'the risks with the negative aspects of diversity of staff are therefore relatively small, since the need for communication on the job is limited. But the benefits are relatively small too. Goods production is determined for the most part by the given production process and affords no scope for creative change in the short term.'

However, this is not the case for service production, which involves a higher degree of adaptation to the customer and the outside world compared with goods production. Although much service production aims, like goods production, for a uniform production process – 'McDonaldisation' – it is still the case that in much of service production, meeting with and adapting to the customer affords scope for creativity. Therefore, they argue, entrepreneurs in service production evaluate the diversity package of opportunities and risks more closely than do entrepreneurs in goods production. 'Deliberation over the work team's composition is therefore a more important issue to the service-producing than to the goods-producing firm, deliberation in which the need for the opportunities of ethnic diversity is weighed against the risks involved.'

The third heading is the *output* from the organisation, for example goods and services. With regard to output variables, better customer service, increased market knowledge and contact, and better image in society, can all be the effects of increased ethnic diversity in a firm. Looking at the example of Sweden, they conclude from the assortment of firms which cultivate immigrants as a home market that it is in service activities that opportunities for diversity are most clearly discernible. This has to do with the character of service activity, which is often performed in direct contact with the customer. Therefore, they argue, success at the job is more dependent on the seller's knowledge of the customer and the customer's impression of the person who performs the service than is the case in selling goods. From their own observations in Sweden, Broomé et al. conclude that at that time the private sector had generally not yet embraced internal ethnic diversity as a way of accessing the Swedish ethnic minority markets.

The analysis of Broomé et al. provides an understanding of the variables which must be taken into account in order to come to conclusions about the positive and negative effects of ethnic diversity in organisations, and guards against idealistic overstatements such as 'diversity is good for business'. With regard to the internal functions of the organisation in particular, they warn:

It first has to be realised that the good aspects of ethnic diversity do not come alone but are *always* accompanied by the more risky aspects of diversity, such as increased conflicts, worse communication, diminished security and openness, culture clashes and stress. Firms accordingly weigh the good against the bad, which many times turns out to the disadvantage of ethnic diversity (Broomé et al. 2000: 16).

This conclusion is consistent with the analysis of Audretsch and Thurik (2000) who also modify the over-simple 'diversity is good for business' assumption. They argue that there are circumstances when a lack of diversity in a work population can have advantages. To the extent to which individuals in a population are identical, the costs of communication and transactions are minimised, with a higher probability of knowledge 'spilling over' across individuals within the group. However, the disadvantage is that in a perfectly homogenous population, new ideas are less likely to emerge from communication across individuals. Diffusion might be promoted, but not innovation (Audretsch and Thurik 2000: 49). This is because 'reasonable people confronted by the same information may evaluate it very differently, not just because they have different abilities, but because each has had a different set of life experiences which shapes the decision making process' (Audretsch and Thurik 2000: 48). In a diverse group communication may be more difficult, but it is more likely to produce innovation.

This phenomenon has implications according to the predominant mode of economic activity in an economy. Audretsch and Thurik contrast traditional routinised economic activity with knowledge-based innovative activity, and argue that homogeneity is more conducive to routinised economic activity whereas diversity is more conducive to knowledge-based innovative activity. Globalisation has now increased the significance of diversity management for North American and Western European economies. This is because the effect of globalisation has not only been to produce more diverse workforces and markets, but also to shift the comparative advantage of North American and Western European nations away from routinised economic activity towards more 'knowledge based search activity'. In such an entrepreneurial economy, the 'knowledge spillovers' within a diverse work population more than offset the other costs of a heterogeneous population.

A similar message come from a study of Norwegian companies by Berg and Håpnes, who conclude 'it is vital to adopt a critical stance to the most idealized messages in a diversity philosophy' (2001: 6). They provide the example of one company where diversity could be seen as directly relevant to profits, and another where it was irrelevant. In a bakery company with 150 employees of whom 10 per cent were immigrants, they found evidence of how 'diversity pays'. The company was experimenting with product development and innovation, and the immigrant workers were being drawn on because of their different experiences and knowledge about various baking traditions. Their contribution to these new products was positive for the business and had also raised the status of the immigrant employees themselves, who felt that their own backgrounds and culture were now better appreciated and understood. On the other hand, an industrial printing company with about 20 per cent immigrant workforce afforded little opportunity to demonstrate the benefits of a diversity approach. There was no use for employees with different linguistic skills as the bulk of its products were destined for Scandinavia, and the entire production process was automated to a degree that made it difficult to see how ethnic differences could be drawn on and profitably exploited either in the production process or in the organisation of work. In this case the management did hold the view that the company workforce should reflect the ethnic composition of the local community, and they recruited immigrants accordingly, but this was not driven by a diversity philosophy but rather by notions of the equal treatment of people and the fair distribution of work. Berg and Håpnes conclude that 'a shortcoming of many presentations of the "Managing Diversity" perspective is that there is inadequate reflection on the great variation that exists between companies' (Berg and Håpnes 2001: 5).

A further qualification is made by Wise (2000), who emphasises the importance of recognising that 'the diversity which matters' is both *contextual* and *perceptual*. An example of the former is that heterogeneity in the workplace will have different implications in an individualistic society such as the United States as compared to a more collective society such as Japan. The latter refers to the fact that one particular dimension of diversity – e.g. religion – may be salient for work groups in one context, and have no significance at all in another. In the same way, the perceived significance of ethnic diversity may vary tremendously in different contexts (Wise 2000: 12).

Diversity management done badly

The above critiques of diversity management serve to modify the over-optimistic claims and over-generalisations that have been associated with the practice. The next criticisms are of a different order, by people who feel that diversity management has been harmful through its inappropriate application by practitioners.

Bendick et al. (1998: 19) in their review of American anti-discrimination training for the ILO, quote a team of American management consultants:

> In 1995 alone, there were as many as 5,000 self-proclaimed experts selling their wares as diversity trainers and consultants. . . .In spite of its positive intent, it is unrealistic to think that with three to five hours of diversity training, complex sociological and cultural principles could be clearly understood, much less applied to all interpersonal relationships. Social conflict was created from the attempt to deal publicly with sensitive social and personal issues better dealt with elsewhere. . . . Because a large number of diversity trainers were women and members of minority groups, many personal agendas, minority platforms, and social conflicts were frequently major portions of the programme….. White males report that they are tired of being made to feel guilty in every discussion of diversity. They are tired of being cast as the oppressors... In addition members of the group that already felt oppressed left the diversity programme feeling even more vulnerable and victimized (Hemphill and Haines, 1997: 3-5).

A diversity trainer described in the *Washington Post* in 1995 the problems and resentment which arose in companies which had experienced bad diversity training:

> Diversity professionals have brought this upon themselves, when they have been careless and reckless in what they ask people to do, some of it even outrageous … And because

too many employees are beginning to feel these courses cross the line, diversity training – including the good training – is getting a bad name and a very bad impression with the public. (*Washington Post*, 5 February 1995)

Some American commentators hold a somewhat cynical view of the 'diversity industry', which blossomed and expanded quickly in the US during the 1990s. '"Diversity" is the buzzword paying the rent of countless consultants' ... 'Many consultants are wiping the dust off their old (Equal Employment Opportunity Commission compliance) presentations and rushing to the marketplace with "diversity' programs" (cited in MacDonald 1993). There are allegations of hasty, ill-thought out and even counter-productive training. In some cases trainers have been criticised for 'sensitivity sessions' which, for example, reduced a white female participant to tears after she had been highlighted as an example of 'privileged white elite'; other criticisms were aimed at trainers who asked participants to furnish stereotypes – e.g. of Anglo-Saxon males, Jews, Hispanics and blacks – and then encouraged groups of participants to denounce each other (MacDonald 1993: 24). Bendick et al. (1998), describe one bad example:

> For several years, the United States Department of Transportation [DOT] provided the most egregious example of how not to conduct diversity training. In the name of exposing racial and sexual prejudice, DOT trainers continually subjected employees to what amounted to psychological abuse. The sessions, suspended in 1993 after outraged complaints from employees, included a gauntlet where men were ogled and fondled by women. Blacks and whites were encouraged to exchange racial epithets, people were tied up together for hours, and some were forced to strip down to their underwear in front of co-workers. Trainers also verbally abused participants, referring to one obese employee as 'muffin queen' (Bendick et al. 1998: 79).

Some critics have complained that the diversity industry was better at inducing guilt than improving relations. The Washington Post (5 February 1995) describes how in response to cases such as these, one diversity training consultant now specialises in repairing the damage of bad diversity programmes.

However, although these criticisms are damaging, they are still do not constitute a 'fundamental' critique of diversity management, as they do not lead to the implication that diversity management is intrinsically wrong – only that *bad* diversity management is wrong. There are far more serious critiques of the diversity management approach, particularly in its application to ethnic minorities, which do not arise simply from experience of 'bad' diversity management but which are rooted in assumptions which call into question some of the basic principles of its operation.

Equal opportunities critiques

There are a number of critiques of diversity management which stem from quarters that are not unsympathetic to equal opportunities or affirmative action approaches, but which are suspicious of some of the specific characteristics of the diversity management approach to employment equity.

Undermines trade union approaches

In Chapter 4, reference was made to certain opposition to diversity management on the part of some black British trade unionists. The British trade union confederation – the TUC – holds each year a national Black Workers' Conference. This is a conference where issues relating to black/ethnic minority members are aired, with all unions affiliated to the TUC allowed to send representatives. At the 1997 conference the following motion opposing diversity management was passed:

> Conference notes with concern the increasing trend amongst personnel and human resource management practitioners to seek to replace existing equal opportunities polices and procedures with those titled managing diversity or mainstreaming. (…) Both of these stress the perspective of the individual within the employing organisation, rather than focussing on the promotion of equal opportunities strategies, or on challenging discriminatory practices and outcomes.

Accordingly, the Conference called on the TUC Race Relations Committee to support initiatives that expose the inadequacies of 'managing diversity' and 'mainstreaming', and to work with all unions and other organisations that actively encourage effective policies and proposals to improve racial equality.

Consistent with this trade union criticism are the findings of a survey into the range and type of anti-discrimination training in the UK, carried out under the co-ordination of the ILO (see Chapter 3). This found that the responses of *trade unionist* trainees to diversity management training seemed to be more critical than other trainees, with people on trade union courses much more sympathetic to the types of training which are focused more specifically and directly on tackling racist and discriminatory behaviour. In the words of one trade unionist respondent, diversity management was just a new way of 'masking exploitation' (Taylor et al. 1997: 62). As described in Chapter 4, later studies confirmed a general suspicion of, or opposition to, diversity management by British trade union representatives (Wrench 2004; Greene et al. 2005).

One reason for British trade union activists' negative responses may well be precisely because the emphasis on culture could be seen to divert policies away from an anti-racism' or 'anti-discrimination' approach, which in Britain has been associated with a straightforward 'black-white' dichotomy, until recently the dominant paradigm in British race relations. This is at a time when the paradigm is increasingly being questioned: 'Blackness defined as the common experience of oppression by non-whites has given way to a myriad of externally imposed or self-asserted ethnicities' (Ranger et al. 1996: 1). Some commentators deplore this development. Aziz Al-Azmeh sees that 'the recent transition, most specifically in Britain, from structural considerations of immigration to a culturalist notion of ethnic diversity' has had the double effect of 'breaking up the solidarities of oppression and of mystifying a "social reality of stunning diversity"'. False constructs of community, defined in terms of religion/culture have emerged from this interaction of involution and ideology' (Al-Azmeh 1993: 1-3, cited in Ranger et al. 1996: 1). The implications of the trend to pluralistic ethnic identities in the context of diversity management will be discussed in more detail later.

Undermining legal approaches

Another reason why some activists are suspicious of the spread of diversity management is that it might complicate or undermine battles that are still being fought in Europe for stronger legal measures, both at national and EU level against racism and discrimination in employment. These suspicions might be reinforced by the example of New Zealand, where the embracing of a diversity management approach by employers' interests was interpreted as a conscious strategy to avoid the imposition of tougher measures. In the early 1990s a new equal employment opportunities trust was set up in New Zealand with the aim of educating the private sector into 'making the most of a diverse workforce'. In the eyes of many equal employment opportunity practitioners the trust was established in order to enable a back-down from the introduction of potentially tough equal opportunities legislation at a national level. Thus the concept of managing diversity was seen as the acceptable 'soft option' (Jones et al. 2000).

In the early 2000s there were developments in Europe in the direction of stronger legislation against racism and discrimination. In 2000 the EU Employment and Social Affairs Council of Ministers adopted the proposal for an EU Racial Equality Directive, and Employment Equality Directive. As described in Chapters 3 and 4, for the first time member states were required to introduce or improve legislation on this topic, and designate a body for the promotion of equal treatment. National governments were given a three year period to set up bodies for the promotion of equal treatment and establish adequate enforcement procedures and sanctions regarding those who discriminate unlawfully. At the beginning of the process, Lappalainen (2001: 3) observed, 'Hopefully ... there will be an interest in creating not only laws at the Member State level that fulfil the EU's minimum requirements, but laws that effectively counteract discrimination on the basis of irrelevant factors'. However, in its 2005 *Equality and Non-discrimination Report* the European Commission noted that a number of Member States had not met the deadlines for communication of transposition of the Racial Equality Directive to the Commission, and in 2005 the European Court of Justice ruled that four countries had failed to honour their obligations in this respect. *Article 13* of the Racial Equality Directive states that Member States must designate 'a body or bodies for the promotion of equal treatment of all persons without discrimination on the grounds of racial or ethnic origin', one of whose tasks should be to provide independent assistance to victims of discrimination in pursuing their complaints about discrimination. It seems that there is a great deal of variety in the degree of power that member states have given these specialised bodies in practice. Whilst some have given powers to their specialised body going further than those set out in the directive (EUMC 2006a), others have been criticised for establishing bodies with insufficient resources and powers (e.g. see the ECRI criticism of the Danish specialised body – ECRI 2006). Indeed, five member states had failed to set in place a specialised body by the end of 2005. The question has to be considered as to whether these delays in some cases reflect a low official priority at national level regarding the issue of anti-discrimination. In 2001 Mark Bell had predicted that in practice there was a risk that there would emerge 'diverse and inconsistent' interpretations of the directive, and warned 'The trade off between precision and distortion is a recurrent dilemma in EU law, but it reinforces the need for vigilance in monitoring how Member States transpose the Directive' (Bell 2001: 52). At a time when long-standing arguments for stronger legislation and enforcement measures in Europe are, apparently, at last being heard, there are those who are suspicious about the simultaneous spread of a business philosophy like diversity management which can be drawn on by those who might wish to excuse their reluctance to incorporate EU anti-discrimination law effectively by arguing that 'softer' or minimalist responses will now be adequate.

A soft option

This leads us to another reason why equal opportunities activists are suspicious of diversity management, namely the fear that diversity management might be used to prioritise 'soft' rather than 'hard' equal opportunities practices. The problem is that diversity management in practice can mean many things. It can be little more than a desire to celebrate cultural diversity, or it can incorporate the full range of previous equal employment opportunities and affirmative action measures. As we have seen with the typology in Section 3, we can conceive of a range of different levels of anti-discrimination and equal opportunities measures in organisations, with at the 'soft' end measures such as the recognition of cultural differences at work, and at the 'harder' end the setting of targets, the use of positive action, or even the adoption of some forms of preferential treatment. It is possible that diversity management can be used to give the impression that an organisation is doing something for excluded groups whilst avoiding many of those aspects of anti-discrimination and equal opportunities activities which are likely to be less popular with employers. For example, employers might be more receptive to the provision of 'cultural awareness training' and less receptive to positive action measures such as targets to produce a workforce which reflects the ethnic make-up of the locality, anti-discrimination training to modify the behaviour of white managers and employees, or strong internal anti-harassment initiatives. If a diversity management approach consists of little more than celebrating cultural diversity, it will sidestep many of the 'harder' elements which have existed within a broader equal opportunities and affirmative action approach.

In the US there is evidence that there was a back-tracking towards softer measures amongst American employers at a time when affirmative action was first under attack in the US, and when diversity management was taking off. Kelly and Dobbin note that during the late 1980s, although employers were maintaining their procedural safeguards against discrimination and their EEO/AA staff, they curtailed their most proactive affirmative action measures, with fewer special recruitment programmes for women and minorities than there had been ten years earlier and fewer special training programmes. There were also fewer employers with affirmative action plans. They argue:

It seems clear that employers have reduced their commitment to the targeted recruitment and training programs that they adopted in the 1970s under the OFCCP's[2] guidelines for affirmative action. These were among the most aggressive efforts employers made on the behalf of women and minorities, but they were among the most likely to face legal and political challenges and employee backlash, and thus became candidates for deinstitutionalization. (Kelly and Dobbin 1998: 981)

Kelly and Dobbin raise serious questions as to what the long-term consequences of this change will be, and whether the 'weakened version of affirmative action' found in current diversity management practices will do anything to improve the prospects of women and minorities in the future, particularly in the light of a 1995 study which showed that diffuse diversity policies and programmes were much less effective than measures that specifically target women and minority groups (Konrad and Linnehan 1995).

Dilution of the ethnic focus

Another concern amongst equal opportunities activists is that diversity management dilutes policies against racism and ethnic discrimination by mixing them with policies relating to other groups. Sometimes the extension and inclusiveness of the concept is taken so far that it becomes almost meaningless.

Mor Barak (2005) notes that many diversity trainers as well as human resource managers have readily embraced the 'broad' approach 'because it allows them to pull everyone in the organisation under the "diversity umbrella", thus avoiding the controversial process of identifying groups with or without power, those who are discriminating and those who are discriminated against …' (Mor Barak 2005: 130). She describes how, during a diversity seminar in California, she observed a diversity trainer enthusiastically encouraging participants to identify the qualities that made them 'diverse', which included not only characteristics such as race, gender, age, sexual orientation, and disability but also attributes such as the region where they grew up, the high school they attended, and even their hair colour and taste in clothing and foods (Mor Barak 2005: 121). For Mor Barak, this approach represents a common confusion between benign differences and differences that have practical or even detrimental consequences in people's lives. She emphasises that there is a fundamental difference between attributes that make a person a unique human being and those that – based on group membership rather than individual characteristics – yield negative or positive consequences.

> It is important to note … diversity is about belonging to groups that are visibly or invisibly different from whatever is considered 'mainstream' in society. In short it is about being susceptible to employment consequences as a result of a one's association within or outside certain social groups. (Mor Barak 2005: 122)

For Mor Barak, the very characteristic of the broad definition of diversity that some find so appealing is also its limitation. By including all types of individual

---

2   Office for Federal Contract Compliance Programs.

differences as 'diversity', the implication is that *all* differences are equal and therefore trivialises those differences. The main criticism is that such expanded definitions reduce diversity to benign differences among people, thereby diluting the serious consequences of prejudice, discrimination, and lack of power that were clearly associated with the original set of diversity characteristics. (Mor Barak 2005: 130).

However, even when the concept is simply extended to other groups who have suffered exclusion, and is not over-extended to embrace benign and trivial differences, there are still criticisms made of this 'inclusive' approach. The inclusive approach is often what makes diversity management popular with employers. For example, according to one major UK retail employer, the diversity approach has made equal opportunities easier to sell within the company: 'When the emphasis was on gender and race, many employees felt excluded. Now with a broader and more inclusive agenda, the policy is accepted as just being about people and what is best for the business' (*Equal Opportunities Review* no. 81, September/October 1998). But a strength from one perspective is a weakness from another. Critics say this does not allow for the fact that some groups have suffered historically from much greater prejudice and exclusion than others. Some have been marginalised for generations with strong and negative social meaning attached to the traits they possess as a group, and this will not necessarily be the same for all those groups considered to fall into the diversity calculus.

In the US the vice-president of the National Association of African Americans in HR stated that 'You dilute (race), and you'll be pushed back down the ladder because you've got other groups that are competing for the spotlight' (Grossman 2000). In the same article a management professor from Arizona State University also argued that diversity takes away from race – 'If I were trying to significantly improve race relations, I would not advocate such a broad approach.' Daniels (2001) complains that the move to diversity 'pushes race to the fringes'. She gives the example of Federated Department Stores in America whose diversity initiative six years previously covered two groups, women and minorities, and now covers 26, including seniors, homosexuals, atheists, and so on. How can African Americans and other minorities benefit, she asks, when the same human resource chief who handled just two programmes now administers 26? In America there are those who see diversity's broad approach as a tactic to de-fuse the black struggle for employment equality precisely because it was the 'race' angle which was most unpopular with employers. Thus, for example, the diversity chair of the Society for Human Resource Management was quoted in its journal as saying that race was a 'sacrificial lamb' to launch diversity and make it palatable to corporate America. 'And who is corporate America? White males. And they don't want to hear about race' (Grossman 2000).

The broader diversity arguments are softer, more acceptable than the old arguments, yet some activists in the US oppose them for precisely this reason, given that the reasons for the old arguments still remain – the fact the some social groups suffer far more discrimination and denial of opportunities and general social injustices than others. For example, in 2001, when defending in a federal court its practice of admitting minority students with lower test scores, the University of Michigan did not use traditional arguments regarding social justice and race and ethnicity. Instead it argued that it was benefiting white students by providing them with a diverse educational environment containing large numbers of minority students. A spokesperson for the university stated 'Race matters in our admissions process. It matters because we know when we bring together a diverse student body, we get educational benefits' (*USA Today* 6 February 2001). The American academic Amitai Etzioni saw this approach as somewhat disingenuous, arguing that 'Michigan and company would do best if they stuck to "old" arguments. Some social groups suffered – and are still suffering – from gross injustices' (*USA Today* 6 February 2001).

The diversity approach has been criticised for allowing people to choose the parts of the diversity mix that they like, and under-emphasising or disguising what they don't like. However, the precise content of what is liked and not liked can change in different contexts. When in different circumstances it is the gender angle which is unpopular, then a diversity discourse can underplay this too. Berggren (2000) describes how in the late 1990s there was increasing pressure put on the Swedish armed forces to improve the representation of women. In particular the Swedish government made it clear how dissatisfied they were with the low proportion of women officers. However, this was in the context of what Berggen describes as 'a very strong opinion among men that only men can serve in the armed forces', a resistance which was found at all levels in the armed forces. Thus, Berggren argues, there was a need for an internal discourse to neutralise the threatening external discourse. He states 'As the Armed Forces realised that it soon had to take actions on the issue of their minority problem, that is the question of gender integration, it became important to redefine the meaning of minority.' Unless the meaning of minorities within the Armed Forces was redefined to meaning something else than gender, the Armed Forces would be forced to take actions to actually increase the numbers of women in their ranks, something they wished to avoid. In this context 'A trend in contemporary management literature was the concept of diversity, which suited the Armed Forces purpose extremely well'. Instead of focusing on gender only, they chose to focus on diversity in terms of factors such as race, ethnicity, age, and professional background. Therefore a project which originally had aimed to produce a change in attitudes among male officers in order to increase the number of female officers ended up with discussions about 'how good it is when cultures in general and ethnical cultures in particular meet' (Berggren 2000: 9). The reason why this is unproblematic for the armed forces is that in reality there is no ethnic diversity within the armed forces, so everyone can agree that multi-ethnicity is a good thing. For Berggen the problem with the concept of diversity is that allowed those in power to define what aspects of diversity are relevant, and those that are not.

The gender example shows that there is no logical reason why it should always be 'race' or ethnicity which is underplayed, although the literature suggests that in practice these are the aspects which are most likely to be unpopular with employers. It is more accurate to say that a diversity approach with its mix of categories is likely to be seen as potentially undermining any binary division – black/white, male/female, etc. – which makes it politically unpopular with activists who are fighting on that particular frontier. This can be seen in New Zealand, where the mode of thinking about ethnic difference in organisations was one of bi-culturalism, based around a metaphor of partnership between the Maori and majority population. Thus in this case too, the onset of diversity management and the associated 'multi-cultural' approach was seen as a threat by Maori equal opportunities practitioners (Jones et al. 2000).

Moral arguments

One rather profound criticism of diversity management is that it removes the moral imperative from equal opportunities actions. Arguments for the introduction of equal opportunities and affirmative action policies relate to equality, fairness and social justice. Critics argue that diversity management has moved equal opportunities away from a moral and ethical issue and turned it into a business strategy. Miller (1994) sees this in the context of the push by management consultants to reconstitute equal opportunities in the management language of the 1990s. For Miller, the shift from an equality to a diversity perspective is symptomatic of a de-politicisation of social relations in much of the management consultancy literature on equal opportunities. 'This remoulding of equal rights to capture and contain it within a market model has all but expunged the political meaning of positive action' (Miller 1994).

Whilst this development is seen as an advantage by many people, in that it increases the likelihood of the adoption of the policies by employers, others see it as a long term weakness. The problem is that fighting racism and discrimination will now only be seen to be important if there is seen to be a business reason for doing it. With a diversity management approach, racism is indeed argued to be unacceptable, but only when it is recognised that the outcome of such racism leads to inefficiency in the utilisation of human resources. If a change in market conditions means that racism and discrimination do not lead to inefficiency, then there will be no longer any imperative to combat it. In the American context, Kelly and Dobbin warn:

> Perhaps diversity management will succeed in winning over middle managers because it embraces an economic, rather than political, rationale. But precisely because it is founded on cost-benefit analysis rather than on legal compliance, perhaps diversity management will come under the ax of budget-cutters when America faces its next recession. (Kelly and Dobbin 1998: 981)

An illustration of the potential danger of leaving employment equity initiatives solely to business rationales can be seen in an article in the British newspaper, the *Independent*, in 1993 entitled 'Employers prepare to ditch equal opportunities at work'. The article refers to the main employers organisation in the UK, the Confederation of British Industry, and quotes a 'confidential report' by senior CBI officials which suggested that the CBI was preparing to abandon support for equal opportunities because 'rising unemployment has reduced the need for employers to concern themselves with getting previously under-represented groups into the labour force and improving their levels of skill.' Previous CBI policy had been based on a report in the 1980s which had predicted a 'demographic time bomb' which would lead to a shortage of young people in the labour market. The new report stated that the demographic time bomb had now been defused, with the result that 'Clearly some of the business arguments for accessing and advancing previously excluded groups ... become less relevant' (*Independent* 14 February 1993).

The difference is that equal opportunity legislation, and the legal endorsement of positive/affirmative action, were introduced as means of social engineering, in order to produce a more equitable society. In contrast, diversity management is an organisational policy with business motives. If it is adopted widely it may *indirectly* produce a more equitable society as a side consequence of the actions of individual companies. But in theory, within any individual organisation, it could just as easily work in the opposite direction, and produce the opposite effect. We can see this if we use the parallel example of women in management, taking the example of a Swedish case study (Sundin 2000). Sundin describes a retail company consisting of small stores selling sweets, newspapers, tobacco, flowers and other general goods. Employees are mainly women, who fill the posts of shop managers and the regional sales managers who form the link between the individual shops and the district central office. The company initiated a diversity policy to enhance the 'competence and flexibility' of the company. Given the existing female dominance, one of the immediate goals was therefore to recruit more men. By a diversity management logic this could produce the benefits of a more diverse and possibly creative workforce. However, at the same time it could go in the opposite direction of a national goal to improve the proportion of women in management and higher status occupations and thereby produce a more equitable society. A national or local government policy of positive/affirmative action could put pressure on an individual employer to set targets for the long term recruitment of more women managers, in pursuit of the social goal of a more equitable society. However, as the Swedish case study shows, it is possible to conceive of an organisationally-based diversity policy which operates in precisely the opposite direction.

Thus, although some see the use of diversity management as an acceptable substitute for more 'political' interventions such as affirmative action, others see this as a more worrying development which reflects a broader trend at a societal level, namely, the intrusion of the market into areas where previously there was action by democratically elected government. As Hobsbawm writes:

> Market sovereignty is not a complement to liberal democracy: it is an alternative to it. Indeed, it is an alternative to any kind of politics, as it denies the need for political decisions, which are precisely decisions about common or group interests as distinct from the sum of choices, rational or otherwise, of individuals pursuing private preferences (Hobsbawm 2001).

For some critics, serious questions must be raised about whether individuals within organisations pursing private preferences constrained by the market can be left to be the custodians of employment equity practice.

Fundamental critiques

The previous point leads to the next category of critiques, the more fundamental criticisms which question the whole basis and existence of diversity management.

Here diversity management is criticised for the fallacy of ethnic reification, and is also attacked for neglecting the structural determinants of inequality, and obscuring and mystifying inequalities of power, with the ideology identified as helpful to economic liberalism and neo-conservative political forces. Most of these critiques can be categorised as left/radical, although there can be found some from a right/ conservative end of the spectrum too.

Reification of ethnicity

One critique is that a diversity management approach is rooted in a major intellectual fallacy, namely the reification of ethnicity. One of the initial appeals of diversity management has been that it takes the concept of ethnic culture and uses it in a positive rather than negative way. Previously, the concept operated to the disadvantage of excluded groups. For example, Soininen and Graham (1995) describe the expansion of new types of job in Sweden which involve the delegation of responsibility, a stress upon individual initiative and a greater reliance on teamwork, leading to an increase in the importance of communication skills and 'social competence'. Some authorities have seen this as an understandable justification for not employing people from other ethnic backgrounds, because, for example, they may lack the knowledge of and familiarity with functioning in a Swedish environment which is part of this 'social competence' (Soininen and Graham 1995).

In theory, a diversity management approach could reverse this. Instead of cultural difference acting as a liability and a barrier to the equal opportunity of ethnic minorities, it could in some circumstances be seen by employers as a desirable trait, and become for the holder a positive asset. However, critics say that the approach of diversity management still operates from an unnaturally exaggerated and reified view of ethnicity and culture. By emphasising the differences of ethnic identities and cultures in the ideology of diversity management there is a danger of simultaneously transmitting and perpetuating a view of the permanence and immutability of cultures and at the same time reducing ethnicity to simplified constructs which can be easily summarised and transmitted in management training sessions. The problem is to recognise at what stage does a genuine desire for sensitivity in treating people from different cultural backgrounds appropriately at work (see Hofstede 1991) turn into unreasonable cultural over-generalisations. For example, an American diversity writer and consultant, Michàlle Mor Barak, writes that research has shown that 'Latinos (both Mexicans and Mexican Americans) are guided by a concern with socioemotional aspects of workforce relations to a far greater degree than are Anglo-Americans' (Mor Barak 2005: 193). Is this the sort of generalisation which should have practical implications for management style? In a 1998 US survey of training in the anti-discrimination/equal opportunities field, carried out under the earlier mentioned ILO programme (see Chapter 3), the researchers found an independent training provider whose training 'describes Hispanics as family oriented rather than work oriented and then explains to employers how they can motivate their Hispanic employees by appealing to these family interests' (Bendick et al. 1998: 79). The potential excesses in taking this approach too far are easy to see. Another American diversity management trainer teaches that blacks 'react quickly to changing situations', as evidenced by their style of playing basketball (*The New Republic*, 5 July 1993). A European diversity management consultant expressed his exasperation at the over-emphasis on culture of origin by some practitioners: 'I've heard of Norwegians going to Palestine just to learn how to treat Palestinians in Norway fairly. This is completely unnecessary – you just need to ask them!'.[3]

Many people argue that it is erroneous and fallacious to regard ethnic cultures as identifiable and unchanging systems of shared values and attributes attached to particular groups. As one Swedish academic put it, when discussing multiculturalism and diversity in Sweden, the problem with diversity management is the 'conservative, essentialised and static' perceptions that become associated with the concept of diversity.

> The existence of differences among people due to their national origin thus becomes an axiom which requires no verification. Furthermore, inasmuch as individuals are still defined in relation to their 'home' countries after two or even three generations, the importance of actual living conditions in Sweden is neglected. This makes the message of ethnic diversity not only static and conservative, but also a message that contributes to essentialising differences on the basis of ethnicity (de los Reyes 2001a: 171).

Critics say that diversity management therefore continues to reify ethnicity and present an exaggerated view of the importance of cultural differences, fallacies which were drawn on as arguments for excluding ethnic minorities in the first place. Furthermore, some people may not wish to be categorised by their ethnic origin. In their study of diversity in Norwegian organisations, Berg and Håpnes observe that some individuals may find it burdensome to be defined as a carrier of particular cultural characteristics. 'In several of the companies we visited, many of the migrants emphasised that they did not at all wish to be "marketed" as very different from Norwegian-born employees' (Berg and Håpnes 2001: 6).

The implicit 'essentialism' within diversity management discourse is one of the points made in a major critique of diversity management by Lorbiecki and Jack (2000). They argue that the view that social identities are fixed and unchanging, as so often implied in diversity management texts, is contested within the academic discourse of cultural studies. They draw on the work of Grossberg (1996) to suggest that notions of the self are inextricably bound up in questions of identity formation and the struggle over two models of the production of identity. The first model assumes that there is some intrinsic and essential content to any identity, defined either by a common origin (e.g. place of birth, racial heritage) or a common structure of experience (e.g. being a woman, black, old, gay or disabled). 'The majority of discourses on diversity management would appear to fall into this category since they commonly use essentialist divisions to signify diversity.' Although there are often contestations against the *negative* images within this mode of identity formation in order to replace sexist, racist, ageist, homophobic or disabled stereotypes with positive ones, as in the early days of the women's and black power 'liberation' movements, this struggle simply replaces one fully constituted, separated and distinct identity with another (Lorbiecki and Jack 2000: 26).

---

3   Personal interview, June 2000.

The second model rejects the possibility of fully constituted, separate and distinct identities based on a universally shared origin or experience and argues that identities are always temporal and unstable. Lorbiecki and Jack argue that although Grossberg's (1996) second model of identity formation paves the way for an appreciation of multiple identities, these identities will still be constrained by certain discursive practices, such as diversity management discourses, which adhere to the notion that identities are monolithic and fixed.

The debate over the nature of identity perhaps constitutes another argument as to why diversity management may find a more sympathetic context in the US than in some European countries. For example, Herbert J. Gans describes 'the re-emergence of symbolic ethnicity' in the US, and writes that larger society seems to offer some benefits for being ethnic. 'Ethnicity, now that it is respectable and no longer a major cause of conflict, seems therefore to be ideally suited to serve as a distinguishing characteristic.' (Gans 1996: 153).

In the debate within sociology and anthropology on the significance of identity and ethnic culture, there are those who criticise the 'primordial' view of ethnicity which has been associated with a traditional anthropological approach. In an article called 'the poverty of primordialism', Eller and Coughlan (1993) write of the fallacy of seeing ethnic phenomenon as things which are ascriptive and inflexible. Far from being self-perpetuating, ethnic identities 'require creative effort and investment'. In other words ethnicity is 'a socially constructed variable definition of self or other, whose existence and meaning is continuously negotiated, revised and re-vitalised'. The primordial approach to ethnicity is 'taking phenomena that are simply "already existing" and "persistent" and reifying and mystifying them into things that are "natural", "spiritual" and "have always existed and always will"' (p. 50). It is therefore a fallacy to see ethnicity and its associated cultural characteristics as 'givens', between which the interactions can be regulated by inter-cultural management or diversity management techniques.

On the other side there are those who argue that it is too dismissive simply to see ethnic identities as some sort of arbitrary false consciousness. They argue that ethnic phenomena are 'real' enough to make it necessary to take ethnicity into practical account, but without going to the extremes of the primordial fallacy. Furthermore, people from different ethnic backgrounds who, under the black/white paradigm, were all put in one category are now recognising a multiplicity of identities, and understanding that 'blackness' is not the only 'mode of resistance' – ethnic identities can also provide cultural 'modes of resistance'. Stuart Hall is one who sees the old 'black/white' dichotomy as no longer adequate. 'It is not possible to occupy black identity at the end of the twentieth century in the heart of Europe in that monological way' (Hall 1996: 113). Whilst Hall would not agree with the simplistic, static and perhaps essentialist view of ethnic identity and culture found in some training manuals for diversity management, he represents those scholars who argue that although ethnic cultural identities are shifting, negotiated and highly contingent, they are nevertheless important phenomena which endure over time and cannot be dismissed as merely superficial and arbitrary. In this sense, to make no allowances for ethnicity in organisational and social policies can be a kind of discrimination.

There are other serious criticisms which relate more to political disagreements over the nature of society. These political critiques can originate either from the Right or from the Left of the political spectrum.

Critiques from the Right

Critics under this heading also tend to be critics of earlier equal opportunity and affirmative action approaches. Lynch (1997) writes:

> The ambitious organization change masters astride the diversity machine have far more in mind than limited reforms. They are extending affirmative action's top-down hiring campaign into a broader multi-cultural revolution in the American workplace and beyond. Both the ends and the means of this policy movement pose a substantial threat to the values of the generic liberalism enshrined in modern American law and culture: free speech; individualism; nondiscrimination on the basis of ethnicity, gender, or religion; equality of opportunity; equal treatment under universalistic laws, standards and procedures; democratic process; and above all, a sense of national unity and cohesion … (Lynch 1997: 32).

Lynch laments the spread of 'the diversity machine's ideology of proportionalism, identity politics and cultural relativism' which he sees as a blend of 'social science and ideology' transmitted and promoted by diversity advocates aided by powerful allies in corporate boardrooms and in the White House. For Lynch, 'Marx's class struggle between the bourgeoisie and the proletariat has been converted to identity politics' cultural war between white males and everyone else' (Lynch 1997: 33). He dismisses the diversity advocates depiction of white male culture, for example, as too simplistic. It confuses 'white male values' with those of the values and norms of the upwardly mobile middle classes across many nations of the world, and at the same time neglects the wide range of variation that exists within the allegedly monocultural white male category. He also sees the demographic projections about the diminishing size of the white American population to be grossly exaggerated. Behind the diversity drives he sees corporate and government leaders and a 'relatively small class of "knowledge workers" or "cognitive elite" who are increasingly distant from the opinions of the masses'. For Lynch, 'The urge to management rationally and assuage morally the tensions caused by immigration, ethnic relations, and social change dates from the Progressive era's fascination with behavioural and scientific reform'. Indeed, 'the urge to mange diversity in specific organisations often masks the urge to manage society itself' (Lynch 1997: 42).

One type of conservative critique comes from those who resist anything which moves away from the old assimilationist, 'melting pot' approaches to American society. An example of this would be that Denton (1997), an American Professor of Management, in his article 'Down with diversity (at least some of it): a case for cultural identity'. Denton emphasises the importance of cultural identity on a national level, and draws on a historical example to make his point. He contrasts the long-lasting Chinese empire, with its emphasis on creating a common cultural identity, with Confucian philosophy at the centre of it, with the short-lived Ottoman empire, whose greatest weakness was that it had no common cultural identity. From this example he concludes 'An empire, nation or corporation that allows diversity can be asking for trouble' (p. 172). For Denton, the recognition and institution of divisions based on different ethnic identities will be a weakness, not a strength, for an organisation. 'Diversity may promote innovation and fresh viewpoints but will ultimately destroy cultural identity' (p. 173).

Critiques from the Left

More common than critiques from the right are those from more of a left/radical perspective, and a common theme in these is that diversity management is an ideology which mystifies and obscures genuine social inequalities and ignores their structural bases. Kersten (2000) argues that diversity management appears to be a progressive development, with organisations voluntarily undertaking to create a diverse and welcoming environment that is supportive to all groups of people. 'In this regard, it is very tempting to join the bandwagon and view diversity management as the final answer to our long-standing national and corporate problems of racism and exclusion.' However, she argues that the fault with diversity management is that it is too simplistic. It presents a model that is relational rather than structural in nature, with its emphasis on aspects such as training, communication, mentoring and teamwork and excluding the more fundamental issues of structural equity and accountability. 'This fails to take into account the deeply rooted nature of racial problems and ignores the extent to which such efforts are influenced by both the organizational and societal context.' She argues that even after diversity management programmes have been implemented, real problems of exclusion, conflict, harassment, and marginalisation continue to exist in organisations. In the diversity approach, the real issue of racism and other forms of systemic discrimination becomes trivialised and minimised. 'Furthermore, diversity theory fails to locate racism in the very structure, ideology and process of the organization and the wider social culture at large. Rather, it presents a deceptively simple and cheerful remedy that covers rather than uncovers the problem at hand, an approach that ultimately may do more damage than good.'

Moreover, Kersten is highly critical of diversity management's 'inclusiveness strategy' that incorporates white males as one of the many groups to be considered. She argues that rather than recognising and dealing with the reality of racism, this strategy simply accommodates the dominant group. 'This parallels the social-political shift in recent American history that seeks to portray everybody equally as "minorities", evident most clearly in the "white ethnic" movement. It also, and similarly, minimizes and denies the real differences in historical and contemporary experiences, and the extent to which "color blindness" is not and never has been a reality in this society' (Kersten 2000: 244). She concludes that diversity management presents a pluralist strategy that celebrates diversity for the 'common economic good', while ignoring the structural and cultural racial biases that exist in the organisation. It offers an apparent unity which obscures the genuine conflicting economic and political interest which exist between various groupings. Therefore, rather than presenting a new movement around differences, 'diversity management represents a new version of a much older racial ideology that seeks to obscure real inequities in favor of a rhetoric of equality' (Kersten 2000: 245). She argues that diversity management must be seen as both reflecting and responding to changes in the larger social and political context in the US. 'The emergence of diversity management has coincided with a general regressive change in the social climate that has included a political and a judicial withdrawal from a commitment to racial equity, as reflected in the renewed political debate around affirmative action, the judicial narrowing of affirmative action application, and the continued struggle around EEO funding.' It is also reflected in the larger social conflict around race, as in, for example, the white male backlash and increasing incidents of racial hatred and violence.

> The emergence and popularity of the diversity management movement can thus best be understood as the outcome of ongoing dialectical tensions that exist in our society – structural, economic, ideological and rhetorical in nature – and rather than resolving these tensions, diversity management offers a new ideological and mediated cultural response designed to contain, restrain and obscure the fundamental racial inequalities that are inherent in our society (Kersten 2000: 245).

Two New Zealand academics who fall into the radical school in their critique of diversity management are Grice and Humphries (Grice and Humphries 1993; Humphries and Grice 1995). Whilst they understand that those who have an interest in employment equity may see the diversity management trend as an 'opportunistic coincidence of organizational needs of business and moral principles of inclusiveness', they caution against the 'seductiveness' of the management of diversity (Humphries and Grice 1995: 18). These writers agree with the earlier mentioned 'moral' critique of diversity management, criticising its move away from arguments of justice.

> The diversity argument is being couched entirely in economic terms and gives us no reason to see diversity management as anything other than an attempt by management to dissociate traditional EEO and AA[4] arguments from arguments of equity and justice. As a consequence, arguments such as 'managing diversity' free up another area of decision making to managerial 'truth' and management prerogative and peripheralise arguments promoted to redress inequity or injustice. (Grice and Humphries 1993:15)

They see that the diversity management exponents, in their desire to distance themselves from AA and EEO, misleadingly represent them as having been 'forms of favouritism not concerned with merit' – which is not the case. On the contrary, they have always stressed merit as a key consideration. (Humphries and Grice 1995: 21-22). By moving the discourse of diversity management away from the discourse of EEO it moves the focus away from categories of people who may be argued to have had a history of exclusion and therefore, by membership of that category, be deserving of some particular attention. The whole question of the *injustice* of the exclusion of anyone on any basis from the access to the security afforded through employment is sidestepped (Humphries and Grice 1995: 15).

> In the light of Foucault's argument that 'discourse is the power which is to be seized' (1984: 110), the shift in language from EEO to diversity presents a much greater shift than is initially apparent. In dispensing with the EEO discourse in favour of that of managing

---

4   i.e. 'equal employment opportunity' and 'affirmative action'.

diversity, we are effectively rejecting the historical lineage of the EEO discourse in favour of the managerialist diversity and, as such, providing support for the particular interests in favour of such discourse. Where EEO may be seen as an attempt to address the inequity of exclusion, managing diversity represents an attempt to maintain as many vestiges of this past exclusion as possible (Humphries and Grice 1995: 22).

However, the privileges of inclusion may be delivered to a more diverse group than in the past. The context of this is the New Right discourse of laissez-faire in relation to government activity, and a complete faith in market principles, so that external non-business constraints promoting equal opportunities are seen as illegitimate. In response to diversity theorists such as Thomas (1990), who states that previous equal employment opportunity and affirmative action polices which have focused on group membership are 'unnatural', they argue:

> To Thomas, affirmative action is referred to as 'unnatural' because it interferes with the 'natural' functioning of a market comprised of competitive individuals aspiring for upward mobility. What Thomas doesn't say is that the categories natural and unnatural are equally the products of discourse. Anything can be defined natural or unnatural if you are in control of the parameters by which that categorising is based. The market is held up as the ultimate natural while things like intervention based on an ethical argument is held up as decidedly unnatural. (Grice and Humphries 1993: 17)

Thus despite having an appearance of concern with fairness, equality of opportunity and empowerment, 'the economic argument underlying the discourse of managing diversity is unlikely to reduce the systematic disenfranchisement of groups of people from access to employment opportunities and economic security' (Grice and Humphries 1993: 22). Where inequality has been historically structured into social and employment relationships, and where a group has been systematically confined into low paying jobs for generations, then group structured inequalities in education and employment will simply persist over time. Only positive or affirmative action policies, it is argued, will shift this, rather than a 'celebrating diversity' approach.

In their second paper they argue that the individualising of diversity management in the move away from the categories associated with traditions of affirmative action and equal employment opportunity fits well with the trend to economic liberalism and the move in industrial relations away from trade unions and collective bargaining. Humphries and Grice quote a representative of the New Zealand Employers Federation who argues that the focus on categories of people in the tradition of EEO and AA is outdated, and that people who are traditionally associated with such categories are better off pursuing success on an individual basis. For example, she argues, women are able to negotiate contracts which suit their individual and family circumstances. Humphries and Grice counter that, on the contrary, 'evidence from other OECD countries ... indicates that gender equality is most likely to occur where there is high union density, centralization of wage fixing, and public expenditure on active labour market policies' (Humphries and Grice 1995: 21).

They argue that the management of diversity is more consistent with a liberal economic discourse precisely because it does not attempt to categorise people in the way found so unproductive by such interest groups such as the New Zealand

Employers Federation. Because the focus is not on equalising differences between groups but on responding to individual needs and aspirations, human diversity can be linked more closely to HRM models of labour control (Humphries and Grice 1995: 24). The management of diversity purports to value individuals as people while at the same time minimising their social identification with specific categories of alienated people. 'This is a mental precondition for the acceptance of new social divisions between the core and the periphery. Responsibility is to ones self, the competitive individual, not to a group who may be (collectively) excluded. Loyalty is to be given to the employer, not traditional EEO categories of race or gender ....' (Humphries and Grice 1995: 30).

Although, under the banner of diversity management, the advances of previously excluded people into diverse occupations may be heralded by some as achievement of equity, 'all is not what it seems. Advances into the managerial ranks by a limited number of women is no reason for optimism.' They agree with Calas and Smircich (1993: 77) that the increased opportunities for some individual women (perhaps achieved through the celebration of the very characteristics which once justified their domestication) may be 'particularly useful ways to pacify emotionally the vast majority of workers ... who will have to adjust downward their expectations of better pay under globalisation'. Humphries and Grice conclude that:

> We are concerned that in the rapidly globalizing discourse of liberal capitalism 'the discourse of equity' is being replaced with 'the discourse of diversity'. We fear that 'the discourse of diversity' is the discourse of pragmatics clothed in the garments borrowed from 'the discourse of equity'. It is time to reclaim the garments. ... Contemporary preferences for an economic pragmatism in the promotion of EEO and AA may mean that in the future communities may have little or inappropriate labour regulation and limited practice in public resistance to unfair exclusion from employment opportunities and the social necessities which increasingly are derived from them (Humphries and Grice 1995: 31).

A number of 'radical' American critics of diversity management are brought together in the volume *Managing the Organizational Melting Pot: Dilemmas of Workplace Diversity* by Prasad et al. (1997). Cavanaugh makes a point also made by many others in the volume, namely that you cannot understand diversity management without understanding the present day American political context, in this case the 'neoconservative racial project of "colour blind" racial politics and "hands off" policy orientation' (Cavanaugh 1997: 38). He argues that it is diversity's 'near-fabulous quality' that attracts suspicion. 'How much faith can be invested in a discourse that assumes away, and thereby exempts from critique, the systemic nature of racial and gender construction in the contemporary workplace and American society at large ?' (Cavanaugh 1997: 40).

For Cavanaugh, the concept of diversity provides management with an effective way to re-establish its competency. It says to important outside groups that business is out in front on the multicultural question because the new diverse workplace can be achieved without the conflict and politics associated with affirmative action. 'In this way, workplace diversity aligns management thinking with the current "live and let live" policy orientation favored by powerful neoconservative interests'. The concept of diversity is useful because it has an inclusive and generous feel to it, suggesting a transcendence of sectional interest. And possibly most important, it resolves the problem of "Otherness", which functions to 'reassure management itself that it is still in the saddle' (Cavanaugh 1997: 40). Therefore, 'celebrating workplace diversity' can be understood as a pre-emptive ideological project that aims to neutralize race and gender (the Other) before current demographic trends politicize them' (Cavanaugh 1997: 44). Cavanaugh asks the question:

> will the denial of the structural power imbalances that is called for in this thin psychological attempt to cure intolerance ... hasten the demise of racial and sexist hierarchies or operate to sustain them? Because of the suspicion that power-free discourses operate to separate the political and the economic (Giddens, 1991), it seems a bit premature to equate celebrating differences with celebrating equality (Cavanaugh 1997: 44).

The important point about a diversity management ideology is that although diversity may not always appear to 'work' at one level (the instrumental), it can still be understood as smoothly operating on quite another (the symbolic) (Cavanaugh 1997: 34).

Lorbiecki and Jack (2000) use critical discourse analysis as the basis of their critique of diversity management. They start by quoting definitions of diversity management from the US and the UK which indicate that diversity management is an instrument or tool that uses people's diversity as the means of achieving economic goals – helping organisations survive, enhancing their economic performance and making a profit. The instrumental use of these diverse 'human resources' to achieve these organisational goals is only possible through mechanisms of control or compliance. In order to demonstrate how diversity management operates as an instrument of control or compliance Lorbiecki and Jack use critical discourse analysis to provide a reflexive interpretation of the definitions of diversity management.

They argue that critical discourse analysis yields a deeper understanding of diversity management by providing a socio-political interpretation of the words that are used. 'This form of critical analysis conceptualizes words and sentences as micro-level forms of discourse, which index macro-level expressions of power relations within society as a whole'. This form of analysis, they argue, is useful in critiquing diversity management because it enables us to ask: 'who is being constructed as different? For what purposes? And with what consequences? But more fundamentally, it tells us something about the power processes invoked in the management of difference' (Lorbiecki and Jack 2000: 23).

One of the definitions of diversity management they analyse comes from Kandola and Fullerton (1998: 8), quoted earlier in Chapter 1:

> The basic concept of managing diversity accepts that the workforce consists of a diverse population of people. The diversity consists of visible and non-visible differences which will include factors such as sex, age, background, race, disability, personality and workstyle. It is founded on the premise that harnessing these differences will create a productive environment in which everybody feels valued, where their talents are being fully utilised and in which organisational goals are met.

Lorbiecki and Jack state that in this definition diversity is presented as being about fixed differences, 'thus suggesting that there can be no movement either within or across visible or invisible boundaries.' They then turn to the use of the verb *harnessing,* normally used to describe the action of placing a bridle or rein on a horse, which is used in this text 'as an index for the control of *everyone* so that none can escape.' The text then ends with organisations as the stated beneficiaries, 'but who within them is to be better off: those managing diversity or those being managed?' (Lorbiecki and Jack 2000: 23). From their analysis of this and other definitions of diversity management, Lorbiecki and Jack identify a number of critical points regarding diversity management, its meanings and notions of difference.

> First, managing, or management, is presented as the privileged subject which sees diversity as an object to be managed. Distance is therefore created between 'those who manage' and 'those who are diverse', so that they are split into two distinct groups, with the properties of diversity being located solely amongst 'the managed'. Second, drawing a boundary around 'the managed diverse' group, allows diversity to be identified and controlled as it is located in one space, and it this group that subsequently bears the stigmatization of difference (oppressed groups). Third, masking out the diversity of 'those who manage' is also a control mechanism because it serves to erase any questionable human differentials within this powerful group (Lorbiecki and Jack 2000: 23).

Thus debates on diversity, though couched in the language of tolerance, are really about managing the negative side effects of *undiverted and unaccepted diversity* (p. 24), but from the point of view of the most economically and politically privileged segments of society, who are, in the USA and the UK, 'traditionally members of the white, male and non-disabled dominant group.' (Lorbiecki and Jack 2000: 23–24).

One thing common to the 'left' critiques of diversity management is the focus on the variable of power. A position consistent with this is taken by the Dutch author Koot (1997). He also sees that a 'celebration of diversity' approach can simply serve to mask genuine inequalities of power and interest. Koot states that diversity management theorists 'want us to believe that it is better to start from differences, to accept these, and thus end up in harmonious collaboration. In my opinion, this point of view is rather idealistic, patronizing, and at times counterproductive. If differences are interrelated with inequality relations, tolerance ... boils down to accepting the status quo' (p. 334).

The reality, according to Koot, is that 'Those in power are usually in favour of tolerance and the less powerful simply want to have more power' (p. 316). In his view the way to reduce 'cultural distance', is not to emphasise, delineate and allow for differences in culture but concentrate on differences in power and conflicting interests (Koot 1997: 334).

Similarly, after presenting an overview of diversity management practices, Nkomo (2001) asks:

> Is diversity management really just talking about respecting all individual differences? If so, this is problematic and cannot in its present form lead to inclusive organisations. There is a real danger in seeing differences as benign variation among people. It overlooks the

Chapter 6

Diversity Management and Anti-Discrimination

As shown in Chapters 3 and 4, there is wide variety in activity within Europe regarding organisational measures for breaking down barriers to the integration of ethnic minorities and immigrants into employment. Diversity management is becoming increasingly embraced in more countries, and more organisational initiatives are attracting the label 'diversity management'. In order to help us understand the variety of responses in different countries it was decided, at the risk of some over-simplification, to set out a classification of levels or stages of anti-discrimination activity in organisational measures, the six-fold typology, leading up to the stage of diversity management. The typology can provide a point of reference for understanding and classifying activities, and a basis for comparison of these activities between different national contexts.

A number of questions have been generated in the context of a growing interest in diversity management in Europe. For example, what are the implications of the differences between the US – the 'home' of diversity management – and the EU, and in the differences within Europe itself? What are the implications of the critiques made of diversity management from various quarters?

Diversity management and combating discrimination

Given the nature of many of the critiques of diversity management, one issue in particular to be further explored must be the status of diversity management as an anti-discrimination activity. As we saw in Chapter 5, some critiques of diversity management accuse it of constituting a retrograde step with regard to combating discrimination against immigrants and ethnic minorities. These criticisms have two dimensions – firstly, that diversity management is weak on fighting discrimination because of the nature of its intrinsic characteristics, and secondly, that diversity management can be used by certain interests to undermine alternative forms of anti-discrimination activity. The first criticism objects to a (perceived) emphasis on 'soft' approaches, such as celebrating cultural diversity rather on the 'harder' equal opportunity and positive action measures, laments the dilution of the ethnic focus with other dimensions of difference, and also objects to diversity management's reliance on business arguments rather than on a moral stance on employment equity. The second criticism warns that diversity management can be used by those who wish to argue that businesses are already responding to ethnic equality issues, and that therefore further national measures such as anti-discrimination legislation are unnecessary.

In order to explore more precisely how diversity management and other organisational approaches stand in relation to anti-discrimination, we need to examine the concept of discrimination itself. The international convention whose object is to prevent racism and racial discrimination is the International Convention on the Elimination of All Forms of Racial Discrimination, (ICERD) which was adopted by the UN Assembly in 1965. The first part of it defines what is meant by racial discrimination:

> The term 'racial discrimination' shall mean any distinction, exclusion, restriction or preference based on race, colour, descent or national or ethnic origin, which has the purpose or effect of nullifying or impairing the recognition, enjoyment or exercise, on an equal footing, of human rights and fundamental freedoms in the political, economic, social, cultural or any other field of public life (Banton 1994: 39).

However, this definition is rather too broad for our purposes. We need to refine a little more precisely the different types of discrimination that can exist in the sphere of employment, and then see how our six-fold typology of organisational anti-discrimination activity (see Chapter 3) relates to these. One classification of types of employment discrimination has been suggested by Williams (2000). She conceptualises four main types of discrimination – direct or intentional discrimination, statistical discrimination, societal discrimination, and structural discrimination, with the final category sub-divided into three further types: indirect, past-in-present and side-effect discrimination. Building on Williams work, and adapting it in the light of the evidence on discrimination from European sources, I would like to suggest a re-organisation of the typology, including the re-naming of one type.

Williams uses the term 'direct or intentional discrimination' to refer to the 'least misunderstood' form of discrimination, namely the exclusion of an individual from opportunities because of group-based characteristics to which stigmatic meaning is attached. I prefer to re-label this as 'racist discrimination', and use the term 'direct or intentional discrimination' as a heading which covers all of the first three types, as the second and third types of discrimination are in fact also both direct and intentional. This then distinguishes these three from Williams' next three types which fall under the heading of 'structural discrimination', defined as forms of discrimination which cannot be reduced to any particular individual's bias or actions.

Classification of discrimination

Thus the new classification of employment discrimination consists of six types:

Direct / intentional discrimination

  (1) Racist discrimination
  (2) Statistical discrimination
  (3) Societal discrimination

Structural discrimination

(4) Indirect discrimination
(5) Past-in-present discrimination
(6) Side-effect discrimination

In addition, three further types of discrimination are set out, to encompass other dimensions of employment inequality experienced by immigrant and ethnic minority workers in Europe:

(7) Opportunist discrimination
(8) Legal discrimination
(9) Institutional discrimination

These are explained as follows:

(1) Racist discrimination

This covers actions by racist or prejudiced people who hold and act on negative stereotypes about a social group. In terms of access to work, this is expressed through the refusal to recruit members of a particular social group, and within the workplace this category might be expressed through verbal or physical harassment, or through the exclusion from access to opportunities such as training or promotion. The category is called 'racist discrimination' using the term 'racism' in the broad way that it is often used in practice today. However, some scholars argue that if we want to use it in a more analytically precise way, then we should distinguish between the racist and ethnicist elements of this category. Racism refers to notions of superiority and inferiority according to perceived innate and natural traits of groups, whereas ethnicism is rooted in ethnic stereotypes, prejudices and perceptions of cultural difference, usually with overtones of superiority and inferiority. In reality, practices of discrimination may have elements or mixtures of both types, but it may be important to maintain the analytical distinction between them, particularly when we are concerned with anti-discrimination practices. For example, it has been argued that ethnic stereotypes are more amenable to change by attitude change and educational measures, whereas in the case of practices rooted in racist attitudes, it is probably more important to use social control mechanisms (Heckmann 2001).

Whilst the racist category probably covers the most direct and dramatic acts of discrimination, the ethnicist one can also include the less dramatic, more 'everyday' examples of discrimination. For example, an insensitive or inappropriate handling of cultural differences by colleagues or superiors can have the effect of denying opportunities which are available to the majority workforce. Even these less dramatic forms of discrimination can still have the long-term effect of reducing the opportunities available to minority employees. For example, in everyday workplace interactions, the majority group will often see their actions as culturally neutral, whilst the actions of those from minority backgrounds will be constantly interpreted in terms of their cultural origin. The normality of such frustrating workplace interactions can eventually lead to workers from ethnic minority backgrounds holding back from taking initiatives or from contributing to group decision-making processes.

(2) Statistical discrimination

This covers actions which are based not on personal racism or on prejudices about a particular social group held by the discriminator, but on perceptions of the minority group as having certain characteristics which will have negative consequences for the organisation. An employer might reason that on average the productivity of a particular gender or minority group is known to be lower, and although the range of capabilities and talents within this group is varied, the employer is unable to differentiate, and therefore finds it convenient to treat all alike. When an employer eliminates from consideration a candidate from a group which is not perceived to be as 'profitable' as other groups, it is argued that such an attitude is a reflection of rational economic behaviour and is not to be confused with racism (for a discussion of this argument see de los Reyes 2001b: 106–107). However, as Williams states, there may be a 'fine line' between statistical discrimination and the first type of discrimination because often the employers' assumptions about statistical tendencies in a particular group are incorrect. Nevertheless, it does constitute a qualitatively different category of discrimination to the previous one. For one thing, in this category the characteristic associated with the group could in theory be a positive rather than a negative trait – for example, a group may be seen as exhibiting an above average tendency for entrepreneurship, which may be seen as rendering them less inappropriate for the jobs being offered. Nevertheless, 'even when the assumptions are borne out by the evidence, statistical discrimination treats individuals not on their merits but on the basis of group characteristics, and so violates the liberal principle of equality' (Williams 2000: 64).

(3) Societal discrimination

This is actions based on the fact that although a person may be free of hostility or prejudice, he or she is aware that *other people* have negative attitudes towards members of a social group. If employers are aware that there is potential prejudice against an ethnic minority group amongst valued customers, they may avoid recruiting or promoting members of that group into a position where they will be in direct contact with these customers, such as sales representative. If employers know that a section of the workforce would be resistant to working alongside a member of an ethnic minority group, they may avoid hiring a member of that group to work in that section. If employees of an employment agency know that immigrants would not be welcomed by a particular employer, they may avoid sending an immigrant to be interviewed for a vacant position.

The differences between the above three types of discrimination can be illustrated simply by the three following examples. For racist discrimination the argument might be 'I won't employ Indians because they are all lazy'; for statistical discrimination it might be 'I won't employ Indians because they will go off and start their own businesses', and for societal discrimination it might be 'I won't employ Indians because my customers won't like it'.

(4) Indirect discrimination

This is where apparently 'neutral' recruitment practices or work routines in practice discriminate against members of an ethnic group, e.g. recruiting employees through their family connections to the (predominantly white) current workforce. (If such practices are truly inadvertent they may be regarded as structural discrimination; alternatively, the practices could be disguised forms of direct discrimination of Type 1, 2 or 3.) Indirect discrimination is most easily understood with regard to recruitment, when, for example, an unnecessary minimum height restriction for a particular job may militate against women, or against certain minority groups that originate from a part of the world where people are on average shorter. In the context of the workplace, this heading could also include the passive adherence to company rules or traditions which do not allow for changed circumstances in the workforce. A rule of 'last in, first out' when redundancies are made will disproportionately penalise an immigrant workforce of recent duration. Even the perpetuation of traditional practices such as inflexible dress codes, canteen menus or holiday rules can be potential factors of indirect discrimination in the context of a new multi-ethnic workforce. As was stated in Chapter 3, the implication of cultural diversity in a workforce may mean that 'systems and procedures that are appropriate for some groups may be inappropriate or actually discriminatory if applied to other groups of people' (Stewart and Lindburgh 1997: 14).

(5) Past-in-present discrimination

This is where 'neutral' practices have greater negative impact on a minority group because of *historical*, rather than current, intentional discrimination. Williams describes this as 'among the most pervasive and pernicious sources of structural discrimination' (Williams 2000: 65). For example, if past discrimination has confined minority group members to inferior jobs, then patterns of structured inequality will persist over more than one generation even after the current discrimination has been removed.

(6) Side-effect discrimination

This is when discrimination in one social sphere will generate inequality in another social sphere, even when there is no discrimination in the second sphere. For example, discrimination in housing or education can have repercussions for inequality in the sphere of employment.

Additions to the typology of discrimination

In addition to the six types in the above classification, there are two other types of discrimination, which are not always conventionally seen as discrimination. These might be labelled 'opportunist discrimination' and 'legal discrimination'. Finally, there is the broad concept of 'institutional discrimination'.

(7) Opportunist discrimination

This is differential treatment, and possible exploitation, based not necessarily on the racism or prejudice of the employer, but on the knowledge that the minority ethnic group is in a weak position in society and in the labour market (perhaps because of the effects of racist or past-in-present discrimination, or the kinds of legal discrimination described below) and can therefore can safely be given inferior working conditions, paid lower wages, etc. (such as. the exploitation of legally restricted or undocumented workers, as described in Chapter 4). This type of discrimination does not apply to exclusion at the recruitment stage, as some employers are only too willing to recruit such exploitable workers in this category.

(8) Legal discrimination

This is the kind of discrimination which was described in Chapter 4, and is found more in some European countries than others. Whilst European anti-discrimination law confers the right to labour without discrimination, including for third country nationals, there are legal restrictions within some countries which restrict the access of non-nationals to certain (often public sector) occupations, or the use of permits which restrict their ability to change jobs. Laws and administrative restrictions governing the access of third country nationals to employment are in principle legitimate, unless it can be proven that discrimination has taken place on the grounds of ethnic/ racial origin. Nevertheless they are instruments which do contribute to inequalities along the lines of social group membership, and are considered by some to be a form of 'legal discrimination'. For example, in some European countries even long-term immigrant residents can remain on a range of restrictive work and residence permits, which severely limit their freedom in relation to majority workers.

(9) Institutional discrimination

It is argued that where some progress has been made in measures to fight direct and open discrimination, there remains a residue of racial inequality which is understood to be partly the result of more subtle, structural institutional forces rather individual acts of exclusion by identifiable persons. The terms 'institutional racism' or 'institutional discrimination' are sometimes used to cover this. There seems to be a great variety in what different actors mean when they use such terms. Some people simply see 'institutional racism' as any racist behaviour which takes place in institutions, rather than by an isolated individual. Others have equated institutional discrimination with 'indirect discrimination', or used it simply to mean 'legal discrimination'.

The term 'institutional racism' was first used by black power activists in the US in the 1960s. It is argued that what characterises '*institutional* racism' is an emphasis on *consequences* rather than intentions, on *regular* and *routine* discrimination rather than occasional, and on *practices* and *structures* (Williams 1985). In the UK the term was thrust into public gaze by the Macpherson report in 1999 into inadequate police response to a racist murder, which concluded that the police had been 'institutionally racist'. Macpherson defined this as 'the collective failure of an organisation to provide an appropriate and professional service to people because of their colour, culture or ethnic origin', which 'can be seen or detected in processes, attitudes and behaviour which amount to discrimination through unwitting prejudice, ignorance, thoughtlessness, and racist stereotyping which disadvantages minority ethnic people' (Macpherson 1999).

The first question that needs to be raised concerns the difference between 'institutional racism' and 'institutional discrimination', and how these relate to 'structural discrimination'. In 2005 the Swedish government presented the results of an inquiry into structural discrimination in Sweden regarding ethnicity/religion (Lappalainen 2005). In this report 'structural discrimination' is defined thus:

> Structural discrimination … refers to rules, norms, routines, patterns of attitudes and behaviour in institutions and other societal structures that represent obstacles to ethnic or religious minorities in achieving the same rights and opportunities that are available to the majority of the population. Such discrimination may be either open or hidden, and it could occur intentionally or unintentionally.

The report goes on to define structural discrimination as a term which also covers 'institutional discrimination'. Furthermore, it goes on to argue that in the USA and the UK the term 'institutional racism' is used to describe the same phenomenon. Therefore, at least for the Swedish report, 'structural discrimination', 'institutional racism' and 'institutional discrimination' are basically the same thing.

Yet few academics would argue that 'racism' and 'discrimination' are the same thing. It is generally acknowledged, for example that you can have racial discrimination without there being a 'racist' motive or ideology behind it. Should not therefore 'institutional racism' have more of a component of racist intention, motive and ideology than institutional discrimination does? Yet just the opposite seems to be the case if look at the definitions of 'institutional racism' (Macpherson) and 'structural discrimination' (Sweden). Macpherson's institutional *racism* allows '*unwitting*' prejudice, whereas the Swedish report's structural *discrimination* could occur '*intentionally*' or unintentionally.

It is clear that there remains some inconsistency in the everyday use of these terms. One solution might be to clarify things by abandoning altogether the use of the term 'institutional racism'. Indeed, as O'Grady et al. write, 'how can an institution be racist, as it is not capable of action/thought/belief in the way that people are?' (O'Grady et al. 2005). These authors argue that the way that racism and race ideas become regularised in routines of action does not illustrate 'institutional racism', but rather '*institutionalised* racism'.

This leaves the term 'institutional discrimination' specifically for practices at the organisational level which have discriminatory outcomes, but which may not necessarily be driven by conscious racist beliefs. The term becomes a broader, over-arching one and is therefore not the same as the others in the classification. What can be labelled 'institutional discrimination' within an organisation is likely to be rooted in a combination of the types set out in the classification – for example, it might include racist discrimination by some people with racist ideas, there may be unthinking 'ethnicist' cultural over-generalisations, there may be routine 'societal' discrimination carried out by people with no racist attitudes, but simply following traditions of recruitment, there may be routine practices of indirect discrimination, a failure to understand and make allowances for 'past-in-present' historical discrimination, and all this could occur in a national context of broader legal discrimination. All of these might come together over time to characterise the organisation's common practices, and may go so far as to constitute part of an organisational culture.

Does diversity management address these types of discrimination?

Having distinguished between a variety of types of discrimination relevant to the area of employment, the next issue to consider is whether and how diversity management addresses these. The research commissioned by the EU and the ILO in the 1990s (see Chapter 3) identified practices which could be clearly classified as *racist, statistical, societal, indirect, opportunist* and *legal* discrimination in EU labour markets and workplaces. Does a diversity management approach address the full range of types of discrimination, and does it do so more or less effectively than the anti-discrimination activities at other levels in the organisational typology set out in Chapter 3. We should first remind ourselves of the classification:

1. Training the immigrants/ minorities
2. Making cultural allowances
3. Challenging racist attitudes
4. Combating discrimination
5. Equal opportunities policies with positive action
6. Diversity management/ mainstreaming

In reality diversity management policies can include all of the elements of these different levels, or only a few. It was noted earlier that some 'diversity management' policies seem to consist of little more than celebrating cultural diversity, and there are questions as to whether these types can be classified as an 'anti-discrimination' measure. Whilst some companies apparently see the core of their 'diversity' activities as making some sort of cultural allowances (level 2), this type of activity can be categorised as 'anti-discrimination' only inasmuch as it covers some of the elements of *indirect* discrimination. Direct anti-discrimination activities should ideally include the organisational activities categorised at levels 3, 4 and 5. Some diversity management policies do include the various anti-racist or combating discrimination methods at these levels. Clearly, organisational activities at levels 3, 4 and 5 are those which directly address racism and discrimination, and elements of these taken together can in theory cover *racist, statistical, societal* and *indirect* discrimination. Relevant to *side-effect* discrimination would be some of the organisational initiatives described in the *Gaining from Diversity* report in Chapter 3 (Stewart and Lindburgh 1997), which included examples of activities *outside* the spheres of employment and the labour market. These could be community initiatives by companies in schools, or in community development programmes. Similarly in the European Compendium of Good Practice (Wrench 1997a) there was an example of an Italian employer who instituted an initiative to counter discrimination in the housing market on behalf of the company's immigrant employees (Carrera et al. 1997). Such initiatives are in effect tackling *side-effect* discrimination – the employer recognises that discrimination against immigrants in the sphere of education or housing is having a direct negative impact on their employment opportunities or conditions. When various elements of racism and discrimination crystallise over time into an organisational culture of *institutional discrimination* this is precisely what diversity management proponents claim in the long term it should be able to address, as ultimately the goal of a diversity management policy is to produce a new organisational culture.

We saw in Chapter 3 indications from the European projects of the 1990s to suggest that the most common components of policies which employers identified as 'anti-discrimination' or 'diversity' activities at that time were actions at level 1 – 'training the immigrants/minorities'. Is such training to be classified as an 'anti-discrimination' measure? A first reaction is to argue that it is not. The simple provision of, for example, language training, is not normally considered to be an anti-discrimination activity. In most European countries it seems that providing language and other training for immigrants has been the first organisational response to the arrival of immigrants. Not only is this not normally classified as tackling discrimination, it often reflects just the opposite – a lack of consciousness of the problem of discrimination. It can occur as part of an implicit 'deficit' approach, which sees ethnic inequality as primarily a human capital 'supply-side' issue, and often goes with an unwillingness to recognise and address the 'demand-side' problem of discrimination. In this context, such training activities are generally not classified as 'anti-discrimination'. However, further reflection suggests that in some circumstances a 'training the immigrants/ minorities' component within an equal opportunities or diversity management policy can be classified as anti-discrimination, depending on the context and the underlying rationale. There are a number of reasons why a broader definition of 'anti-discrimination' may embrace this activity.

Firstly, if a lack of language ability results in lack of power in the labour market and a restriction of the ability to resist exploitation by moving to better employment, then the reduction of this power deficit by language training can be seen as tackling *opportunist* discrimination. Furthermore, language training might be understood as *indirectly* tackling racism in the longer term. For example, if a language or educational deficit results in members of a minority group being over-represented in inferior work or amongst the unemployed, then training can promote their broader and better employment, thereby tackling the roots of racism, and thereby *racist discrimination*, by undermining the idea that visible minorities are second-class citizens suited to second-class jobs.

Secondly, economic and organisational restructuring increasingly means that immigrant workers in Europe need language and communication skills that they did not require 20 or 30 years ago. If at a time of organisational restructuring a lack of language skills is used as an excuse to make redundant the immigrant workforce, then the provision of language training in this case can be defined as 'anti-discrimination', in this case anti-*indirect*-discrimination.

Thirdly, there is another way in which providing skills training for immigrants or ethnic minorities can be defined as anti-discrimination. If it forms part of level 5 activity, i.e. a positive action training programme, openly justified as a means of going further than the 'level playing field', as a way of compensating for past historical discrimination, then in this sense it is anti-discrimination, i.e. anti-*past-in-present* or historical discrimination.

Is diversity management weak on positive action?

The above point leads us to a more specific criticism of diversity management – that its weakness as an anti-discrimination measure is above all rooted in its lack of components which address the form of structural, historical discrimination known as *past-in-present* discrimination. What is the point of celebrating a diverse organisational culture when the long-term effects of historical exclusion mean that under-represented minorities are not in a position to take advantage of opportunities to join, or progress within, the organisation? The sort of position which attracts these criticisms is characterised by the authors of what is probably the best known textbook on diversity management in the UK, Kandola and Fullerton (1998). They emphasise that they see no place for group-targeted positive action or affirmative action in a diversity management approach. 'Our view is that an approach whose underpinning philosophy is the needs of the individual will automatically be compromised when any actions are based purely on someone's supposed group membership' (Kandola and Fullerton 1998: 125).

If this philosophy represents an intrinsic aspect of diversity management, then the criticism that it is weak on measures against structural discrimination is indeed a serious one. However, it seems that this stance is not necessarily shared by all diversity management practitioners and advocates. For a further insight into a basic division within diversity management approaches we can turn to the work of Liff (1997). Liff starts with the question 'Is managing diversity a way of repackaging equal opportunity, strengthening it or undermining it?' Part of the difficulty in answering that question lies in the 'struggle for ownership of the term managing diversity by those from competing perspectives.' To help us understand the different versions of diversity management she first clarifies the previous equal opportunities approach. Underpinning this is the importance of treating people equally, irrespective of their sex or ethnic origin. However, to eliminate discrimination and promote equality it can be acceptable to recognise social group differences. These can be expressed in positive action measures to counter the effects of current or past discrimination.

Such measures try to ensure that everyone has the opportunity to compete on the same basis, but ultimately they aim to produce a situation where the individual's race or sex is of no significance in regard to their treatment and access to opportunities.

In contrast, managing diversity does encourage organisations to recognise differences. However, there is more than one approach to this. One way is to see differences as more or less randomly distributed between individuals, and the other is to see the characteristics as related to, for example, membership of an ethnic group. Thus there are two main approaches to managing diversity. The first is where social group equality is not accorded any specific significance as an object of organisational policies, and where diversity includes a whole range of things, not just ethnicity and gender. This is called the *dissolving differences* approach.

However, there is another approach to diversity management – the *valuing differences* approach – which acknowledges socially-based differences, and allows policies which recognise gender or ethnicity. 'These policies acknowledge socially-based differences and their significance for the perpetuation of inequality' (Liff 1997: 14). This type could therefore very easily embrace some of the initiatives at other levels in the six-fold organisational typology, such as extra training for under-represented groups, and positive action measures or even targets for the recruitment of under-represented minorities. Practitioners using this type argue that the problem with the individual approach is that 'It allows for social difference but as yet has no well developed strategy for dealing with ways in which job structures and personnel practices have been shown to disadvantage women, ethnic minorities and others and to advantage white males systematically' (Liff 1997: 23).

Thus we can see that the diversity management approach has more variety than some critics acknowledge. And this also explains why some of the critiques set out in Chapter 5 seemed contradictory. Some were criticising a diversity management approach which they assumed to be the individualistic *dissolving differences* approach, and others were criticising a diversity management which they assumed to be group based *valuing differences* model. As an example of the former, the New Zealand critics of diversity management stated: 'The problem is that there is no room for group claims with 'managing diversity', let alone claims for indigenous status as a difference which makes a major difference. Nor is there room for a collective, rather than an individualised concept of identity.' For these authors the problem is that 'the vocabulary of managing diversity reduces all difference to equivalence' (Jones at al. 2000: 369).

Yet it is clear that for some versions of diversity management this is not so. In practice diversity management may attempt to embrace both the individual and group dimensions. For example, there was a rather illuminating quote in an online debate hosted by the Chartered Institute for Personnel and Development, the professional organisation in the UK for personnel and human resource managers. In response to the question 'What is your definition of diversity?' a director of human resources replied:

> There are a number of definitions to describe diversity in the work environment. Primarily they fall into two categories: one focusing on the 'individual' and providing equality and fairness to every person, and a second focusing on 'group', for example, 'women' or

'ethnic minority', where the provision of equality and fairness is recognised in terms of meeting the needs of groups. (...) The challenge in the work environment is for diversity to mean valuing difference (all people are valued in their difference) while at the same time addressing 'group' characteristics and stereotyping, since many of the procedures, practices and employee behaviours that directly or indirectly discriminate are around stereotyping groups.[1]

Clearly this shows that in practice diversity management can be more complex and more flexible than many of its critics imply, and that its particular form in specific contexts must therefore be the subject of empirical investigation. For some observers, diversity management is a practice that distances itself from many of the earlier levels or stages, breaking itself from its roots in an entirely new approach, and carried forward by business dynamics. Others see it as simply a logical and more ambitious extension of earlier stages. Examples of the latter are Kirton and Green, authors of a UK diversity management textbook, who conclude from their reading of the existing research-based literature that 'most academic commentators are sceptical about "managing diversity" as linked to "business case" arguments for equality and the ability of this approach to redress material inequalities. This is because of the contingent and partial nature of business case arguments with their reliance on the functional rationality of management ... as drivers of employment policy' (2000: 7). Two British consultants who were interviewed for this report saw no necessary contradiction between the moral and business arguments. One of them, when asked whether she saw the 'business' or 'moral' argument as predominant, replied 'You must use the two together. You can't use diversity on its own. It is sterile'.[2] In the words of Kirton and Greene, (2000: 7) 'It ... remains important for diversity policy levers to grow from and on to existing equal opportunity policies, rather than replace them'.

The relationship of diversity management to equality legislation

The second order of criticism of diversity management with regard to its relationship with anti-discrimination activities is that it can be used by those who wish to argue against other levels of activity, such as anti-discrimination legislation. Again, we can see here that there is more variety in reality than critics allow for, and there are different views as to whether a diversity management approach is intrinsically incompatible with, a replacement for, or can co-exist with, strong legal and administrative measures for equality. The origins of the fears come from outside Europe. As we saw in Section 5, in the US context diversity management was interpreted by some as an acceptable 'toned-down' substitute for equal employment opportunities and affirmative action measures, which were then under political attack. In New Zealand it was seen as way of circumventing the demand for equity legislation before such legislation was introduced. Thus there are those who fear a similar syndrome in Europe. Yet it is by no means certain that diversity management is *intrinsically* incompatible with a strong

---

1 PM Online debate, www.peoplemanagement.co.uk.
2 Personal interview, February 2002.

legally-based approach, and some European commentators see the co-existence of diversity management and legal equality measures as not only possible but highly desirable. Unlike in the US, diversity management in Europe was taking off at a time when political opinion had moved towards *stronger* legal approaches, as reflected in the new EU directives (see Chapter 4). For some European commentators there are 'thorny questions' about the easy co-existence of the two approaches (Glastra et al 1998: 173), but at least, they argue they do not necessarily exclude each other. As one UK director of human resources stated: 'Diversity in organisations does need to be supported by legislation. This introduces a common minimum standard across organisations and indeed ensures an element of consistency in practices followed by organisations working in the same marketplace'.[3]

The European diversity management consultants who were interviewed for this report saw no contradiction between diversity management and strong anti-discrimination legislation. The UK consultant, herself from a earlier background of employment in a major UK company, emphasised the importance of legal pressure and employment tribunal cases in stimulating the adoption of diversity management policies, and welcomed the new EU directives as 'a good way of getting things through the door'.[4] Those who talked about the spread of diversity management in the Netherlands and Sweden were clear that at that time the main driving force was labour shortages. However, there are times and circumstances when this driving force may not be there, and some SMEs in certain sectors are not at all worried about labour shortages. Hence there was a perceived need for other forms of external pressure. These can provide the initial stimulus for diversity management which, when it is adopted, may then proceed under its own momentum. It is not insignificant that in the case of the American companies who were surveyed by Wentling and Palma-Rivas (see Chapter 2), all stated that their diversity programmes had started originally because of the pressure of the Civil Rights Act or movement, and the need to comply with affirmative action requirements.

The spread of diversity management could prove to be a stimulus for getting employment equity issues on to the agenda in Europe in places where more traditional approaches would not have been successful. However, the wider adoption of diversity management does not serve as a substitute for efforts to improve the legislative context on employment equity. Diversity management policies are not a replacement for strong and properly enforced legislation on access to employment and numerical representation. They should exist alongside, and contribute themselves to, anti-discrimination measures, but there are areas which still need to be covered by legislation. This will be addressed further in the final chapter.

---

3   PM Online debate, www.peoplemanagement.co.uk.
4   Personal interview, February 2002.

Chapter 7

Diversity and the Future

Most literature on diversity management focuses on the internal processes of the organisation, and explores the implications of diversity management policies (or their absence) for the organisation's workforce, clientele and markets. In contrast, this book has devoted its attention primarily to the external environment of the organisation, namely factors within the European national and EU contexts which have potential implications for the development and character of diversity management in Europe.

The book began with an examination of diversity management in the US, looking at the factors behind its growth and the nature of its practices. It then moved to the European background context for the development of diversity management, focusing specifically on the relevance for immigrants and ethnic minorities, and raising questions about a number of significant differences between the US and Europe. In the light of Point and Singh's observation that 'Most studies of diversity appear to have been undertaken in the United States, where there is a very specific cultural, social and historical context' (2003: 752), the aim has been to present examples of how some of these factors of cultural, social and historical context differ in Europe and may have direct implications for the nature and form of diversity management there.

Chapter 2 listed factors which are regarded as having stimulated the development and adoption of diversity management in the US. Whilst many of these apply equally to companies in a European context, some of them clearly do not. Chapter 3 drew on the limited cross-national work that had been carried out in Europe in the 1990s (usually by international bodies like the ILO or European Commission) to illustrate the lack of awareness of employment discrimination in many countries at that time, despite the growing evidence, generally provided by researchers, that racial discrimination in employment was a serious problem. In some countries there was a total absence of consideration of the issue, and where the problem was being addressed, there was evidence of some national differences in emphasis. Overall, the most common approach to employment inequality in the 1990s in Europe seemed to be policies to remedy the perceived deficit within the immigrant or minority populations. Diversity management was still a very a marginal activity. All this was a very different context to the US, where diversity management was the latest in a long history of organisational-level initiatives related to anti-discrimination and employment equity for minorities. Before the advent of diversity management there had existed for many years measures such as anti-discrimination legislation, federal contract compliance and affirmative action which had already improved the employment opportunities for members of previously under-represented groups (Allen 2000). In Europe there had been nothing to compare with the laws and practices of the strength and variety found in the US. The degree of variance in experience of policy initiatives in this field *within* Europe was far greater than within the US.

The discussion in Chapter 4 led to a number of questions. Will there be a long-term convergence of organisational practice across Europe towards diversity management, because of commonly experienced economic and demographic forces? Or will national emphases of diversity management practices vary according to cultural and institutional differences, different traditions in dealing with immigration and ethnic diversity, differences in previous experiences of organisationally-based equal opportunity policies, or even differences in the quality of national political discourse on immigrants and multiculturalism?

Chapter 4 identified some trenchant criticisms of diversity management emerging from diverse European actors. Thus, Chapter 5 presented an overview of critiques of the practice from both within and outside Europe, made by commentators ranging from those who are sympathetic, to those who are sceptical or downright oppositional. It showed that opposition to diversity management could come from those who are associated traditionally with both the left and the right in terms of political perspective. Whilst the critiques come from a wide range of different standpoints of academics, diversity practitioners and equality activists, one theme within a number of them was a questioning of the value of diversity management for combating racial or ethnic discrimination.

Chapter 6 thus explored further the concept of discrimination and suggested a conceptual clarification which could be used to indicate how different elements within a diversity management policy have the potential to address discrimination of different kinds. It also showed how some critiques have been based on the assumption that there is one particular model of diversity management, when in fact there are significant disagreements between diversity practitioners and consultants about what constitutes the essential properties of a diversity management policy, and what its relationship should be to the various levels of anti-discrimination activity, including the stronger forms of positive action.

The use of typologies and the diversity of diversity

There is clearly a great diversity in diversity management in both theory and practice, and the precise form it takes will depend on the particular perspective of its advocates, set amongst the constraints and enablers of broader factors of historical, cultural and institutional context, and encouraged or discouraged by political activity, both in the action and discourse of local and national politicians, and the activities of grass roots activists. As Prasad and Mills (1997: 18) observe, 'How workplace diversity is understood will, at any given time, depend on culturally relative, historically changeable, social interactions that are developed within contexts of political interaction and struggle'.

One device used regularly in this book to aid the comparability and understanding of different types of organisational policies is that of the typology. Such classifications are attempts to group activities which have internally some consistency with each other, and externally some theoretically significant differences with activities in other categories. These then provide a reference point which can facilitate the comparison of various forms of organisational activity. Some of the typologies employed in this book had already existed, some have been modified and some are new. One new typology is the six-fold classification of organisational anti-discrimination activities. This helped to illustrate the differences between a diversity management approach and other employment equality strategies, and show how some initiatives relating to immigrants or ethnic minorities can be wrongly classified as an organisation's 'diversity policy'. For example, we saw in Chapter 3 a company whose 'managing diversity' policy consisted of language training arrangements, recognising the dietary requirements of religious minorities, and allowing longer periods of unpaid leave to enable non-European workers to take longer vacations when visiting their home countries. These fall into level 1 and level 2 activities in the typology, and therefore are incorrectly classified as a diversity management policy.

Clearly there are policies which go under the heading of diversity management which, if adopted in some contexts, would be identified as regressive in terms of the fight against discrimination, and in other contexts would do nothing to get combating discrimination on the agenda in the first place. It is possible for the positive discourse of diversity management to be used to mask the absence of activity in anti-discrimination. The circumstances of the use, non-use and abuse of the term diversity management are all areas of serious concern. It is a relevant question as to whether the misuse of the term diversity management simply reflects well-meaning ignorance, whether it is related to specific factors of national context, or whether it serves the sectional interest of a particular occupational or political constituency.

Whilst there is evidence that diversity management is steadily spreading in Europe, there is a danger that the lack of previous experience of anti-discrimination policies in some countries will mean that forms of diversity management which develop there will be restricted to the feel-good 'celebrating cultural diversity' types. A policy which, in terms of the six-fold classification, consists only of a combination of levels 1 and 2 – that is, training minorities and making cultural or religious allowances at work – coupled with some of the ideological elements of level 6 – such as stressing the positive value of cultural diversity – is an unsatisfactory and incomplete type of organisational response to ethnic diversity.

The discourse of diversity

The recognition of such dangers with diversity management is not the same as saying, as some critics argue, that diversity management should on principle be avoided and resisted. One problem with some criticisms of diversity management has been an over-reliance on critical analysis of the terminology and discourse. There is only so much significance that can be attached to a discourse analysis alone, and this is best tempered with data from observations, investigations and case studies. For example, in Chapter 5, reference was made to a critique of diversity management as an instrument of 'control or compliance' (Lorbiecki and Jack 2000), based on the analysis of terms like 'harnessing' found in definitions of diversity management. The word 'diversity' itself is judged as signifying 'fixed difference' with no possible movement across physical boundaries. Diversity management critics also point to the use of the word 'management' itself as an indicator of one-sided power and control. Yet the problem of critical discourse analysis is that it may attribute too much significance to words and metaphors. Case studies and interviews with practitioners reveal a far greater variety and flexibility in reality than that suggested by the words which are seen to be significant by critical discourse theorists. Some business practitioners of diversity management themselves state that they are not happy with the overtones of the word 'management' and prefer to suggest something more democratic. Diversity management texts talk about the flexibility of diversity categories and the shifting boundaries of what is 'the diversity that matters'. Thus the insight produced by the analyses of discourse needs also to be complemented by information on real-world practice. Whether diversity management operates as a subtle way of extending one-sided managerial control, or as part of a drive to increase equality and human dignity at work, is an empirical question, not simply a logical one, nor one that can be derived from discourse analysis alone.

Evidence of change

It is difficult to make authoritative statements about the actual state of diversity management development in Europe. Reference has been made in this book to several attempts at surveys, overviews, and listings of 'good practice' which give clues as to where and how quickly diversity management is being adopted in Europe, but all of these have problems regarding their representativeness, not least because most of them depended on replies from the kinds of organisations which were more likely to be sympathetic to diversity management in the first place. Probably the main observations of the European Commission's 2005 report on diversity management are correct, namely that companies in Europe were making 'steady progress' in the implementation of diversity and equality policies, but also that overall progress was patchy, and that there was little evidence for such activity in the ten new EU member states which joined in 2004 and in those from southern Europe. This is also reflected in the data collected by the EUMC, where reports from 2005 suggested that consciousness and practice of diversity management by companies in the new member states, and in Spain, Portugal, Italy and Greece, was virtually non-existent (EUMC 2006a, 2007). In countries of southern Europe the majority of immigrants have been recruited for low skilled work that was shunned by the majority population, and trade unions have been concerned with issues of exploitation and legal insecurity for these workers. Diversity issues for this population have clearly not been on the agenda, although they may become relevant with the emergence of a second generation aspiring for social mobility.

Legal and administrative pressure

This book has identified a number of factors in the European context which might have negative implications for the development of diversity management. Having said this, there has also been evidence that some elements of these have started to change. One development of great potential significance has been the introduction of the Racial Equality Directive, covering all EU member states. By 2005 the transposition process of the directive had been completed in most member states and was still underway in others. Specialised bodies for the promotion of equal treatment were designated by most member states, in some cases for the first time in their history, and some of these bodies have been given powers to take legal action on behalf or in support of victims of racial discrimination going beyond the minimum standard required by the Race Equality Directive (EUMC 2006a). If these powers are exercised, this will help to further raise public awareness on issues of discrimination and diversity, and could well provide a direct stimulus for employers to look sympathetically at diversity management policies. As stated in Chapter 4, the authors of the European Commission's report on diversity management concluded that it is reasonable to infer that by 2005 the EU anti-discrimination legislation had had a considerable impact in promoting action in this field. In the case of the US, there had been, in addition to anti-discrimination legislation, pressure to develop equality and diversity policies from federal contract compliance demands. Whilst this kind of pressure has also generally been absent from the EU, there are small signs of change. For example, in 2005 the city of Stockholm in Sweden adopted a policy to include anti-discrimination clauses in all of the city's public contracts.[1] In 2006 it was announced that the UK government was considering the introduction of pilot schemes which will see companies questioned on their workplace diversity before being awarded government contracts, with the possibility that they may be asked to show how their figures on black and Asian employees relate to the proportions living in the surrounding area (*Guardian* 7.8.2006).

Statistics of ethnic origin

Another problem mentioned in Chapter 4 was the lack of adequate statistics on ethnic/national origin to assist in identifying and combating employment discrimination. The monitoring of such statistics at an organisational level is a routine part of diversity management policies. Whilst this is generally accepted as normal within such policies in the US and Canada (Goldston 2005; Simon 2005), 'ethnic monitoring' continues to be a controversial issue in many EU member states, with both legal and social barriers to the practice. Nevertheless, there were signs in 2005 that authorities in some EU countries were starting to look differently at this area. Ireland, for example, decided to introduce a question on ethnic origin in its 2006 census. Whilst the most principled opposition to such statistics is found in countries which stress universalistic principles, the exemplar of which is France, there were also signs of change in countries such as France and Belgium. As Schnapper et al. have noted (2003: 17), 'it can be observed that certain countries claim to have universalistic principles but are, as a result of the actual process of the management of diversity, inevitably obliged to take into account the specificities of

---

1   Stockholm municipal council (2005) *Protokoll, sammanträde 2005-01-2,* available at: www.stockholm.se.

various populations.' Another impression gained from cases reported to the EUMC over recent years is that there seems to be a more general willingness in European companies to make allowances for cultural and religious differences (EUMC 2007). Making active allowance for cultural diversity is another characteristic aspect of diversity management policies, indicating that such diversity is positively valued.

Grounds for caution

The above developments might be identified as indications of a more positive trend in Europe with regard to the awareness of racial discrimination, and a more sympathetic environment for diversity policies. On the other hand, there also remain significant barriers of attitude and practice to the development of anti-discrimination and diversity awareness and practices, and there are some developments which point in another, less positive direction. As discussed in Chapter 4, one difference in European countries compared to other countries where diversity management is more common, such as the US, Canada and Australia, is the absence of a historically positive view of immigration in building the nation, and the maintenance of legal restrictions on many immigrant workers. One of the pre-requisites of the equality assumptions which are intrinsic to a diversity management approach must be that the ethnically diverse groups which constitute a particular workforce have the same formal legal status as the majority, are just as free to change employers as the majority, and are not legally constrained from applying for other types of work. Yet, as shown in Chapter 4, the employment rights of large sections of immigrant workers across the EU are not equal to those of the majority in these respects.

In some EU countries the majority of immigrant workers are legally restricted in their activities by work or residence permits. Whilst the EU anti-discrimination directives confer the right to labour without discrimination, including for non-nationals from outside the EU, there are other legal restrictions in some countries which deny the access of non-nationals to certain (generally public sector) occupations. In France and Italy, for example, millions of public sector jobs remain closed to some or all non-nationals. These are instruments which contribute to inequalities along the lines of social group membership, and are considered by some to be a form of 'legal discrimination'. According to an EU directive of 2003,[2] third-country nationals who are long-term residents should have the right to the same conditions of work and employment as nationals. However, by the end of 2005 only a minority of member states had transposed this directive. In a context where a high proportion of immigrant workers are constrained in legally inferior positions, a diversity management approach is less relevant.

Barriers to citizenship

Normally the way for an immigrant to achieve complete equality of rights of access to employment, and other related rights, is to become naturalised. Access to

_____

2   Council Directive 2003/109/EC.

citizenship has always been easier in some EU countries than in others (Bauböck 2006). However, in the first years of the 21st century many EU member states had started to make it harder to access citizenship, and harder for an immigrant to settle down by bringing a spouse into the country. In this period the discourse of politicians wishing to appeal to anti-immigrant populism in Europe became more extreme, and immigrant organisations reported a more hostile climate, with Muslims in particular reporting a significant worsening of their everyday experiences since the terrorist attacks on America in September 2001 (EUMC 2006b).

In some countries politicians have started to question long-held rights to citizenship for the children of immigrants; language requirements for citizenship are being introduced or made more difficult, and mandatory 'integration programmes' are appearing in more and more EU member states' immigration legislation. Even in those countries categorised in Chapter 4 as characterised by a more positive attitude to multiculturalism and a more relaxed attitude to citizenship, there have been changes in a more restrictive direction, such as in the UK and the Netherlands. In some countries legislation is introduced stating that citizenship of those who have been naturalised will be forfeited if certain serious crimes are committed. Some of the proposals go even further in promoting the distinction between people who are born citizens and those who have achieved it through naturalisation. For example, a bill on 'integration' proposed in the Netherlands in 2005 would place strict demands on *naturalised* citizens (immigrants and their descendants) if they receive a social benefit allowance such as unemployment benefit, which would not be placed on the national majority who acquired citizenship by birth. Furthermore, whilst immigrants who have attained citizenship may see their rights diminished, there are others with no citizenship who see their rights maintained or increased on the grounds of being seen as part of the 'ethnic' nation. In contrast with the increasingly demanding requirements made on third country nationals living in the EU is the maintenance or even liberalising of policies regarding people who are 'co-ethnics' – those who descended from nationals of EU countries but who were born and living abroad, perhaps following emigration generations earlier. Some EU countries have policies which give priority to such people access to citizenship even when they have never lived in the country and may not even be able to speak the language. In cases where citizenship is required for access to certain jobs, such people can be indirectly prioritised in the labour market over long-term resident immigrants. (There can even be *direct* prioritisation, as in Greece where a 2005 law restricting some self-employed occupations to those with Greek or EU citizenship made an exception for 'those of Greek ethnic origin' – EUMC 2006a).

Unsympathetic messages

The message given out by these practices, in the context of an increasingly populist and anti-immigrant discourse, is not one which sits easily alongside the main messages of diversity management. The prejudices of a component of the majority population will be confirmed by such developments, and the already-resident immigrant population will be given the message that they are second class citizens.

This is not a context sympathetic to or consistent with a multicultural society and the positive views of ethnic diversity inherent in a diversity management approach. Whilst most of the anti-immigrant rules and proposals are not directly concerned with employment, they do have an effect on the broader climate of discussion, and this can have a practical impact on the adoption of diversity management policies. As was shown in Chapter 4, people working for the adoption of diversity management in Danish companies reported that the strident Danish anti-immigrant discourse could be a very real problem for them, making their job much harder. Similarly, people working for diversity management in Belgium remarked that authorities in national and local government who were running initiatives for the adoption of diversity management were sensitive about doing this with too much publicity for fear of people turning to the far right party, the Vlaams Belang. As one Belgian diversity activist put it 'People are scared to be openly strong on diversity'.[3] The political context has an effect.

In conclusion

This aim of this book has been to point to areas for future observation and research regarding topics which have been somewhat outside the normal sweep of diversity management literature. Inevitably this exercise has had some limitations. Firstly, the comparative consideration of cultural and other differences across the EU has been restricted to national differences, using nation states as the key unit of analysis, when a more ambitious analysis might also take account of the relevant regularities and differences that exist within and across European national boundaries. For some scholars, the nation-state centred paradigm has severe limitations and may no longer be the appropriate one for charting the evolving relationship between new immigrants and their host contexts in Europe (Favell 2003: 14).

Secondly, most of the material for the book was collected before the entry of new member states to the EU in 2004 and in 2007, and so the book is rather biased in its examples towards the pre-2004 EU 15. Within the EU 15 countries the main population groups who have been seen as those most relevant to anti-discrimination and diversity measures are the labour migrants of the three decades following World War II, and their descendants (who generally gain citizenship rights but remain identifiable as minority ethnic groups). In addition, several of the EU 15 countries have begun to experience significant labour migration from countries of the former USSR. In most of the post-2004 new member states there has been no comparable labour migration experienced in the post-World War II era, and no corresponding growth of new minority ethnic communities, with all the 'second generation' issues related to this. However, substantial Roma communities are found in the some of new member states, notably the Czech Republic, Hungary, Slovakia, and the later entrants of Romania and Bulgaria. Whilst the EU's anti-discrimination directives will be of potentially great importance for the Roma in order to help to break the vicious circle of deprivation and discrimination that they experience, the implications of a

---

3   Presentation made at a diversity conference in Madrid in April 2006.

diversity management approach for excluded national minorities like the Roma has hardly been considered in the EU context.

Thirdly, there has been a perhaps disproportionate recourse to material in this book from two of the EU 15 member states, namely the UK and Denmark. That is because the author has lived and worked in both of these countries, and so has had the advantage of being able to draw more readily on first-hand knowledge of the issues. Even so, a focus on some countries more than others may not constitute a serious limitation. The strategy has not been to make comparisons between specific countries as such, but to use selected national examples to draw attention to the kinds of national regularities and differences which might be relevant when considering the development of diversity management in Europe.

A central theme of this book has been the relationship between diversity management and discrimination and the clarification of how the one can address the other. It has been argued that some criticisms of diversity management have been too sweeping, and that the flexibility of its nature means that the right kind of diversity management has at least the potential for improving and mainstreaming genuine anti-discrimination and equality issues to the benefit of previously excluded minorities. As illustrated in the trade union comparison in Chapter 4, in parts of Europe where there has been little historical awareness of racial discrimination in employment and no great experience of anti-discrimination activities, diversity management can be identified by activists as a vehicle for getting these issues onto the agenda for the first time. In the context of positions of 'colour blindness' or the denial of discrimination found amongst European employers and trade union leaders, the dissemination of the discourse of diversity management can be a positive development.

It is clear that diversity management cannot be understood and judged in its US context alone. One of the key differences between the EU and US context is that, whereas diversity management in the US was associated (some would say tainted) with the Reagan presidency assault on affirmative action and a retreat from stronger anti-discrimination approaches, in Europe diversity management has taken off at a time when awareness of the need for anti-discrimination activities is increasing, when EU anti-discrimination directives have been introduced, and when anti-discrimination legislation in member states is either being introduced for the first time, or being significantly strengthened.

Diversity management is not to be seen as a substitute for anti-discrimination measures at national and EU level. For one thing, some kinds of discrimination cannot be tackled by diversity management – for example, 'legal' and 'opportunist' discrimination (see Chapter 6) can only be tackled by changes in the law, not by policies at an organisational level. Addressing these kinds of discrimination would provide a more sympathetic environment for organisational diversity policies. Diversity management is complementary to anti-discrimination laws. Laws provide the context in which diversity management policies are adopted. Surveys of US companies which are now operating diversity management policies with enthusiasm show that the original reason for the adoption of these policies was often the pressure of employment equity legislation or federal contract compliance. Only later did they start to appreciate the organisational benefits of such policies. This is why the EU Racial Equality Directive is important, and why NGOs, trade unions and civil society organisations within member states must be seen to draw on the resulting national legislation to assist victims, as a stimulus to anti-discrimination and diversity awareness on the part of employers. Diversity management operates best in the context of strong anti-discrimination law, and within diversity management policies themselves there must be anti-discrimination elements. Diversity management is a way of mainstreaming anti-discrimination activities, not a substitute for them.

Bibliography

Abell, J.P. (1991) *Racisme, Vooroordeel en Discriminatie: bestrijding door beinvloeding van de meerderheid met niet-juridische middelen.* University of Amsterdam, Amsterdam.

Abell, J.P. (1997) *Case Studies of Good Practice for the Prevention of Racial Discrimination and Xenophobia and the Promotion of Equal Treatment at the Workplace: The Netherlands.* European Foundation for the Improvement of Living and Working Conditions, Dublin, WP/97/44/EN.

Abell, J.P., Havelaar, A.E. and Dankoor, M.M. (1997) *The documentation and evaluation of anti-discrimination training in the Netherlands.* International Labour Office, Geneva.

Adler, N.J. (1997) *International Dimensions of Organizational Behaviour.* South-Western College Publishing, Ohio.

Al-Azmeh, A. (1993) *Islams and Modernities.* Verso, London.

Allasino, E., Reyneri, E., Venturini, A. and Zincone, G. (2004) *Labour market discrimination against migrant workers in Italy.* International Migration Papers 67, ILO, Geneva.

Allen, A.L. (2000) 'Can Affirmative Action Combat Racial Discrimination: Moral Success and Political Failure in the United States' in E. Appelt and M. Jarosch (eds) *Combating Racial Discrimination: Affirmative Action as a Model for Europe.* Berg, Oxford, 23–39.

Arrijn, P. Feld, S. and Nayer, A. (1998) *Discrimination in access to employment on grounds of foreign origin: the case of Belgium.* International Labour Office, Geneva.

Audretsch, D. and Thurik, R. (2000) 'Diversity, Innovation and Entrepreneurship', Proceedings of the conference *Workplace Diversity: A Research Perspective on Policy and Practice.* Brussels, June, School of Public and Environmental Affairs, Indiana University.

Banton, M. (1994) *Discrimination.* Open University Press, Buckingham.

Banton, M. (1996) 'National Variations in Conceptions of Racism' Conference paper, Euroconference no.14, *Racism and Anti-Racism in Europe – New Dimensions.* Sønderborg, June.

Bauböck, R. (2006) *Migration and Citizenship: Legal Status, Rights and Political Participation.* Amsterdam University Press, Amsterdam.

Bartz, D.E., Hillman L.W., Lehrer S. and Mayhugh, G.M. (1990) 'A model for managing workforce diversity', *Management Education and Development* vol. 21 no.4, 321–326.

Bell, M. (2001) *Meeting the Challenge? A Comparison between the EU Racial Equality Directive and the Starting Line* Migration Policy Group, Brussels.

Bendick, M., Egan, M.L. and Lofhjelm, S. (1998) *The Documentation and Evaluation of Anti-discrimination Training in the United States.* International Labour Office, Geneva.

Berg, B. and Håpnes, T. (2001) 'Desiring diversity versus equality: What is good practice to combat discrimination of ethnic minorities in employment?', Paper presented at *Sixth International Metropolis Conference*, Rotterdam, November.

Berggren, A.W. (2000) 'Diversity at the Expense of Gender Equality: A Change of Discourse in the Swedish Armed Forces', Paper presented at conference *Diversity Practice: Diversity Management and Integration. Ethnicity and Gender in Focus.* Work and Culture, Swedish National Institute for Working Life, Norrköping, November.

Blakemore, K. and Drake, R. (1996) *Understanding Equal Opportunity Policies.* Prentice Hall/Harvester Wheatsheaf, London.

Bourdieu, P. and Wacquant, L. (1999) 'On the Cunning of Imperialist Reason', *Theory, Culture and Society* vol. 16 no.1, 41–58.

Bovenkerk, F., Gras, M., and Ramsoedh, D. (1995) *Discrimination against Migrant Workers and Ethnic Minorities in Access to Employment in the Netherlands* International Labour Office, Geneva.

Broomé, P., Carlson, B. and Ohlsson, R. (2000) 'Ethnic Diversity and Labour Shortage: Rhetoric or Realism in the Swedish Context', conference paper *Diversity Practice: Diversity Management and Integration. Ethnicity and Gender in Focus* Work and Culture, Swedish National Institute for Working Life, Norrköping, November.

Broomé, P., Carlson, B. and Ohlsson, R. (2001) *Bäddat för Mangfald*, SNS Förlag, Stockholm.

Brüggemann, B. and Riehle, R. (1997) *Case Studies of Good Practice for the Prevention of Racial Discrimination and Xenophobia and the Promotion of Equal Treatment at the Workplace: Germany*, European Foundation for the Improvement of Living and Working Conditions, Dublin, WP/97/39/EN.

Bryant, C.A. (1997) 'Citizenship, national identity and the accommodation of difference: reflections on the German, French, Dutch and British cases', *Journal of Ethnic and Migration Studies* vol. 23 no. 2, 157–172.

Cachón, L. (1997) *Case Studies of Good Practice for the Prevention of Racial Discrimination and Xenophobia and the Promotion of Equal Treatment at the Workplace: Spain*, European Foundation for the Improvement of Living and Working Conditions, Dublin WP/97/46/EN.

Cachón, L. (1999) 'Immigrants in Spain: From Institutional Discrimination to Labour Market Segmentation' in J. Wrench, A. Rea and N. Ouali (eds) *Migrants, Ethnic Minorities and the Labour Market: Integration and Exclusion in Europe* Macmillan, London, 174–194.

Calas, M. and Smircich, L. (1993) 'Dangerous liaisons: the "feminine-in-management" meets "globalization"', *Business Horizons* vol. 36 no. 2, 73–83.

Carrera, F., Ciafaloni, F. and Mirabile, M.L. (1997) *Case Studies of Good Practice for the Prevention of Racial Discrimination and Xenophobia and the Promotion of Equal Treatment at the Workplace: Italy*, European Foundation for the Improvement of Living and Working Conditions, Dublin WP/97/42/EN.

Castelain-Kinet, F., Bouquin, S., Delagrange, H. and Denutte, T. (1998) *Pratiques de formations antidiscriminatoires en Belgique* International Labour Office, Geneva.

Castles, S. (1995) 'How nation-states respond to immigration and ethnic diversity', *New Community* vol. 21 no. 3, 293–308.

Cavanaugh, M. (1997) '(In)corporating the Other?: Managing the Politics of Workplace Difference', in Prasad, P., Mills, A. J., Elmes, M. and Prasad, A. (eds) (1997) *Managing the Organizational Melting Pot: Dilemmas of Workplace Diversity.* Sage Publications, London, 31–53.

CEC (1993) *Legal Instruments to Combat Racism and Xenophobia.* Commission of the European Communities, Office for Official Publications of the European Communities, Luxembourg.

CEOOR (2005). *Bevraging: Actieve publieke uiting van religieuze en levensbeschouwelijke overtuigingen: Voorstellingen en analyse / Consultation: Expressions actives de convictions religieuses ou philosophiques dans la sphère publique.* Centre for Equal Opportunities and Opposition to Racism, Brussels.

Clark, T. (ed.) (1996) *European Human Resource Management: an introduction to comparative theory and practice.* Blackwell, Oxford.

Colectivo Ioé: M. Angel de Prada, W. Actis, C. Pereda and R. Pérez Molina (1996) *Labour market discrimination against migrant workers in Spain.* International Labour Office, Geneva.

Colectivo Ioé: M. Angel de Prada, C. Pereda and W. Actis (1997) *Anti-discrimination training activities in Spain.* International Labour Office, Geneva.

Collet, P. and Cook, T. (2000) *Diversity UK: A survey on managing diversity in the United Kingdom.* Department of Experimental Psychology, University of Oxford, Oxford.

Cözmez, M. (2002) 'Betriebliche Partizipation und Integration am Beispiel der Ford-Werke Köln, in: Hunger, U. (ed.) *Einwanderer als Bürger. Initiative und Engagement in Migrantenselbstorganisationen.* Münsteraner Diskussionspapiere zum NonProfit-Sektor, Münster, 17–21.

Daniels, C. (2001) 'Too diverse for our own good?', *Fortune.com* 9 July 2001.

de los Reyes, P. (2001a) 'Diversity, Differentiation and Discrimination. A Critical View on Current Strategies and Discourses in Sweden', in M. Essemyr (ed.) *Diversity in Work Organisations.* National Institute for Working Life, Stockholm, 157–176.

de los Reyes, P. (2001b) *Diversity and Differentiation: Discourse, difference and construction of norms in Swedish research and public debate.* National Institute for Working Life, Stockholm.

Denton, K.D. (1997) 'Down with diversity (at least some of it): a case for cultural identity', *Empowerment in Organisations* vol. 5 no. 4, 170–175.

De Rudder, V., Tripier, M., and Vourc'h, F. (1995) *Prevention of Racism at the Workplace in France.* European Foundation for the Improvement of Living and Working Conditions, Dublin.

ECRI (2006) *Third Report on Denmark* European Commission against Racism and Intolerance, Council of Europe, Strasbourg.

Edwards, P., Hall, M., Hyman, R., Marginson, P., Sisson, K. Waddington, J. and Winchester, D. (1992) 'Great Britain: Still Muddling Through', in A. Ferner and R. Hyman (eds) *Industrial Relations in the New Europe*. Blackwell, Oxford, 1–68.

Eller, J. and Coughlan, R. (1993) 'The poverty of primordialism: the demystification of ethnic attachments', *Ethnic and Racial Studies* vol. 16 no. 2, 183–202.

ENAR (2005) *ENAR Shadow Report 2005 – Racism in Denmark*, European Network Against Racism, Brussels.

Esmail, A. and Everington, S. (1993) 'Racial discrimination against doctors from ethnic minorities', *British Medical Journal* 306 March, 691–692.

Essed, P. (2001) 'Difference, Discrimination and Diversity in Dutch Work Organisations', paper presented to *International Cross-cultural Perspectives on Workforce Diversity: The Inclusive Workplace*. Bellagio July.

EUMC (2001) *Diversity and Equality for Europe: Annual Report 2000*. European Monitoring Centre on Racism and Xenophobia, Vienna.

EUMC (2004) *Racism and Xenophobia in the EU Member States: trends, developments and good practice. Annual Report 2003/2004 – Part 2*. European Monitoring Centre on Racism and Xenophobia, Vienna.

EUMC (2005) *Racism and Xenophobia in the EU Member States: trends, developments and good practice. Annual Report 2005 – Part 2* European Monitoring Centre on Racism and Xenophobia, Vienna.

EUMC (2006a) *The Annual Report on the Situation regarding Racism and Xenophobia in the Member States of the EU*. European Monitoring Centre on Racism and Xenophobia, Vienna.

EUMC (2006b) *Perceptions of Discrimination and Islamophobia: voices from members of Muslim communities in the European Union*. European Monitoring Centre on Racism and Xenophobia, Vienna.

EUMC (2007) *Trends and Developments 1997–2005: Combating Ethnic and Racial Discrimination and Promoting Equality in the European Union*. European Monitoring Centre on Racism and Xenophobia, Vienna.

European Commission (2003) *The Costs and Benefits of Diversity*. Office for Official Publications of the European Communities, Luxembourg.

European Commission (2005) *The Business Case for Diversity: Good Practices in the Workplace*. Office for Official Publications of the European Communities, Luxembourg.

Favell, A. (2003) 'Integration nations: the nation-state and research on immigrants in Western Europe', in G. Brochmann (ed.) *The Multicultural Challenge: Comparative Social Research* vol. 22, Elsevier, Amsterdam, 13–42.

Fernandez, J.P. (1993) *The Diversity Advantage*. Lexington Books, New York.

Fibbi, R., Kaya, B. and Piguet, E. (2003) *Le Passeport ou le Diplôme?* Swiss Forum for Migration and Population Studies, Neuchâtel.

Forbes, I. and Mead, G. (1992) *Measure for Measure*. Employment Department Research Series no. 1, London.

Foucault, M. (1984) *The use of pleasure: the history of sexuality vol.2*. Penguin, Middlesex.

Gächter, A. (2000) 'Austria: Protecting Indigenous Workers from Immigrants', in Penninx, R. and Roosblad, J. (eds) *Trade Unions, Immigration, and Immigrants in Europe, 1960–1993* Berghahn, Oxford, 65–89.

Gächter, A. (1997) *Case Studies of Good Practice for the Prevention of Racial Discrimination and Xenophobia and the Promotion of Equal Treatment at the Workplace: Austria.* European Foundation for the Improvement of Living and Working Conditions, Dublin WP/97/34/EN.

Gans, H. J. (1996) 'Symbolic Ethnicity', in J. Hutchinson and A. D. Smith (eds) *Ethnicity.* Oxford University Press, Oxford, 146–154.

Giddens, A. (1991) 'Four theses on ideology', in A. Kroker and M. Kroker (eds) *Ideology and Power in the Age of Lenin in Ruins.* New York, St Martins, 21–23.

Glastra, F., Schedler, P. and Kats, E. (1998) 'Employment Equity Policies in Canada and the Netherlands: enhancing minority employment between public controversy and market initiative', *Policy and Politics* vol. 22 no. 2, 163–176.

Goldberg, A., Mourinho, D., and Kulke, U. (1995) *Labour market discrimination against foreign workers in Germany.* International Labour Office, Geneva.

Goldston, J. A. (2005) 'Ethnic data as a tool in the fight against discrimination', in S. Mannila (ed.) *Data to Promote Equality.* Finnish Ministry of Labour/European Commission, Helsinki, 124–137.

Graham, M. and Soininen, M. (1998) 'A model for immigrants? The Swedish corporate model and the prevention of ethnic discrimination', *Journal of Ethnic and Migration Studies* vol.24 no. 3, 523–529.

Green, N. (1999) 'Le Melting-Pot: Made in America, Produced in France', *Journal of American History* vol. 86 no. 3, 1188–1208.

Greene, A. and Kirton, G. (2003) 'Views from another Stakeholder: Trade Union Perspectives on the Rhetoric of "Managing Diversity"', *Warwick Paper no. 74*, University of Warwick Business School, Coventry.

Greene, A., Kirton, G. and Wrench, J. (2005) 'Trade Union Perspectives on Diversity Management: A comparison of the UK and Denmark', *European Journal of Industrial Relations* vol. 11 no. 2, July, 179–196.

Grice, S. and Humphries, M. (1993) 'Managing Diversity. A wolf in sheep's clothing?', in J. Collins (ed.) *Confronting Racism in Australia, Canada and New Zealand.* Volume 1, Faculty of Business, University of Technology, Sydney.

Griggs, L.B. (1995) 'Valuing diversity: where from … where to?' , in L.B. Griggs and L.L. Louw (eds) *Valuing Diversity: New Tools for a New Reality.* McGraw-Hill, New York, 1–14.

Grossberg, L. (1996) 'Identity and Cultural Studies – Is that all there is?', in S. Hall and P. du Gay (eds) *Questions of Cultural Identity.* Sage, London, 87–107.

Grossman, R.J. (2000) 'Is Diversity Working?', *HR Magazine*, vol. 45 no. 3, 47–50.

Hall, S. (1996) 'Politics of identity', in T. Ranger, Y. Samad and O. Stuart (eds) *Culture, Identity and Politics.* Ashgate, Aldershot, 129–135.

Hammond, T.R. and Kleiner, B.H. (1992) 'Managing multicultural work environments', *Equal Opportunities International* vol. 11 no. 2, 6–9.

Harzing, A. and Van Ruysseveldt, J. (eds) (1995) *International Human Resource Management.* Sage, London.

Hayles, V.R. (1996) 'Diversity training and development', in R.L. Craig (ed.) *The ASTD Training and Development Handbook.* McGraw-Hill, New York, 104–123.

Heckmann, F. (2001) 'Racism, Xenophobia, Antisemitism: Conceptual Issues in the Raxen Project', Paper prepared for EUMC Workshop, Vienna.

Heckmann, F. (2003) 'From Ethnic Nation to Universalistic Immigrant Integration: Germany', in F. Heckmann and D. Schnapper (eds) *The Integration of Immigrants in European Societies: National Differences and Trends of Convergence.* Lucius and Lucius, Stuttgart, 45–78.

Hemphill, H and Haines, R. (1997) *Discrimination, Harassment and the Failure of Diversity Training.* Greenwood Press, Westport, CT.

Hjarnø, J. and Jensen, T. (1997) 'Diskrimineringen af unge med invandrerbaggrund ved jobsøgning', *Migration papers no. 21* South Jutland University Press, Esbjerg.

Hobsbawm, E. (2001) 'Democracy can be bad for you', *New Statesman* 5 March 2001, 25–27.

Hofstede, G. (1991) *Cultures and organizations: Software of the mind – Intercultural cooperation and its importance for survival.* Harper Collins, London.

Hubbuck, J. and Carter, S. (1980) *Half a Chance? A Report on Job Discrimination against Young Blacks in Nottingham,* Commission for Racial Equality, London.

Humphries, M. and Grice, S. (1995) 'Equal employment opportunity and the management of diversity: A global discourse of assimilation?', *Journal of Organizational Change Management* vol. 8 no. 5.

Jamieson, D. and J. O'Mara (1991). *Managing Workforce 2000: Gaining the diversity advantage.* Jossey-Bass, San Francisco.

Jedwab, J. (2005) 'Muslims and Multicultural Futures in Western Democracies', *Canadian Diversity* vol. 4 no. 3, 92–96.

Jenkins, R. and Solomos; J. (1987) *Racism and Equal Opportunity Policies in the 1980s.* Cambridge University Press, Cambridge.

Johnston, W. and Packer, A. (1987) *Workforce 2000: Work and Workers for the 21st Century.* Hudson Institute, Indianapolis.

Jones, D., Pringle, J. and Shepherd, D. (2000) '"Managing diversity" meets Aotearoa/ New Zealand', *Personnel Review* vol. 29 no. 3, 364–380.

Kandola, R. and Fullerton, J. (1998) *Diversity in Action: Managing the Mosaic* Institute of Personnel and Development, London

Katz, J. (1978). *White Awareness: Handbook for anti-racism training.* University of Oklahoma Press, Oklahoma.

Kelly, E. and Dobbin, F. (1998). 'How Affirmative Action became Diversity Management', *American Behavioural Scientist* vol. 47 no. 7, April, 960–985.

Kerr, C. (1983) *The Future of Industrial Societies: Convergence or Continuing Diversity?* Harvard University Press, Cambridge.

Kersten, A. (2000) 'Diversity management: dialogue, dialectics and diversion', *Journal of Organizational Change Management* vol. 13 no. 3, 235–248.

Kirton, G. and Greene, A. (2000) *The Dynamics of Managing Diversity: A Critical Approach.* Butterworth-Heinemann, Oxford.

Konrad, A.M. and Linnehan, F. (1995) 'Formalised HRM structures: Coordinating equal opportunity or concealing organizational practices?', *Academy of Management Journal* vol. 38, 787–820.

Koot, W.C.J. (1997) 'Strategic Utilisation of Ethnicity in Contemporary Organisations' in S.A. Sackman (ed.) *Cultural Complexity in Organisations: Inherent Contrasts and Contradictions.* Sage, London, 315–340.

Kossek, E.E. and Lobel, S.A. (eds) (1996) *Managing Diversity: Human Resource Strategies for Transforming the Workplace.* Blackwell, Oxford.

Kühne, P. (2000) 'The Federal Republic of Germany: Ambivalent Promotion of Immigrants' Interests', in Penninx, R. and Roosblad, J. (eds) *Trade Unions, Immigration, and Immigrants in Europe 1960–1993.* Berghahn, Oxford, 39–63.

Lappalainen, P. (2001) 'The challenges posed by the EU anti-discrimination directives', Paper presented at *Sixth International Metropolis Conference*, Rotterdam, November.

Lappalainen, P. (2005) *Det Blå Glashuset – strukturell diskriminering i Sverige.* Statens Offentliga Utredningar, Stockholm.

Lawrence, P.R. and Lorsch, J.W. (1967) *Organization and Environment.* Harvard University Press, Cambridge.

Liff, S. (1997) 'Two routes to managing diversity: individual differences or social group characteristics', *Employee Relations* vol. 9 no. 1, 11–26.

Lind, J. (1995) *Trade Unions in a Changing Society.* CID Studies no. 14, Copenhagen Business School, Copenhagen.

Lind, J. (2000) 'Denmark: Still the century of trade unionism', in J. Waddington and R. Hoffman (eds) *Trade Unions in Europe: Facing challenges and searching for solutions.* European Trade Union Institute, Brussels, 143–182.

Lorbiecki, A. and Jack, G. (2000) 'Critical Turns in the Evolution of Diversity Management', *British Journal of Management* vol. 11, 17–31.

Luthra, M. and Oakley, R. (1991) *Combating Racism Through Training: A Review of Approaches to Race Training in Organisations.* Policy Paper in Ethnic Relations, no.22, University of Warwick.

Lynch, F R. (1997) 'The Diversity Machine', *Society* vol. 37 no. 5.

MacDonald, H. (1993) 'The Diversity Industry', *The New Republic* July 5, vol. 209 no. 1, 22–25.

MacEwen, M. (1995) *Tackling Racism in Europe.* Berg, Oxford.

MacEwen, M. (ed.) (1997) *Anti-Discrimination Law Enforcement: A Comparative Perspective.* Avebury, Aldershot.

Macpherson, W. (1999) *The Stephen Lawrence Inquiry: Report of an Inquiry by Sir William Macpherson of Cluny.* The Home Office Cm 4262-1.

Makkonen, T. (2007) *Statistics and Equality: Data Collection, Data Protection and Anti-discrimination Law.* Thematic Report of the European Network of Independent Legal Experts in the Non-Discrimination Field, Brussels.

Martens, A. and Sette, K. (1997) *Case Studies of Good Practice for the Prevention of Racial Discrimination and Xenophobia and the Promotion of Equal Treatment at the Workplace: Belgium.* European Foundation for the Improvement of Living and Working Conditions, Dublin, WP/97/35/EN.

Mendoza, S. (2000) 'Fostering Equality: Business takes Action', Paper presented at *High Level Meeting on Achieving Equality in Employment for Migrant and Ethnic Minority Workers*. Geneva, March 2000.

Miller, D. (1994) 'The Management of Diversity: A Big Idea whose time has come?', *Discussion Papers in Work and Employment* no.1, University of Northumbria at Newcastle, Newcastle.

Mor Barak, M.E. (2005) *Managing Diversity: Toward a Globally Inclusive Workplace.* Sage Publications, Thousand Oaks, California.

Morden, T. (1999) 'Models of National Culture – A Management Review', *Cross Cultural Management* vol. 6 no. 1, 19–44.

Mutti, A. (2000) 'Particularism and the Modernization Process in Southern Italy', *International Sociology* vol. 15 no. 4, 579–590.

Møller, B. and Togeby, L. (1999) *Oplever diskrimination – En undersøgelse blandt etniske minoriteter.* Nævnet for Etnisk Ligestilling, Copenhagen.

Nimako, K. (1998) *Voorbij Multiculturalisatie: Amsterdam Zuidoost als Strategische locatie.* Amsterdam.

Nkomo, S. (2001) 'Much to do about diversity: The muting of race, gender and class in managing diversity practice', Conference paper *International Cross Cultural Perspectives on Workforce Diversity: The Inclusive Workplace.* Bellagio, July.

Nour, S. and Thisted, L.N. (eds) (2005) *Diversity in the workplace: When we are equal but not the same.* Børsens Forlag, Copenhagen.

O'Grady, A., Balmer, N., Carter, B., Pleasance, P., Buck, A. and Genn, H. (2005) 'Institutional Racism and Civil Justice', *Ethnic and Racial Studies* vol. 28 no. 4, 620–638.

O'Reilly, J. (1996) 'Theoretical Considerations in Cross-National Employment Research', *Sociological Research Online* vol. 1 no.1.

Parekh, B. The Commission on the Future of Multi-Ethnic Britain (2000) *The Future of Multi-Ethnic Britain.* Runnymede Trust/Profile Books, London.

Penninx, R. and Roosblad, J. (eds) (2000) *Trade Unions, Immigration, and Immigrants in Europe, 1960–1993.* Berghahn, Oxford.

Point, S. and Singh, V. (2003) 'Defining and Dimensionalising Diversity: Evidence from Corporate Websites across Europe', *European Management Journal* vol. 21 no. 6, 750–761.

Prasad, P. and Mills, A.J. (1997) 'From showcase to shadow: Understanding the dilemmas of workplace diversity', in P. Prasad, A.J. Mills, M. Elmes and A. Prasad (eds) (1997) *Managing the Organizational Melting Pot: Dilemmas of Workplace Diversity.* Sage, London, 3–30.

Prasad, P., Mills, A. J., Elmes, M. and Prasad, A. (eds) (1997) *Managing the Organizational Melting Pot: Dilemmas of Workplace Diversity.* Sage Publications, London.

Purkiss, B. (1997) 'Practice makes perfect', *Connections* no.1 CRE, London.

Ramkhelawan, S. (2001) 'Diversity and the Dutch labour market policy for ethnic minorities', Paper presented at *Sixth International Metropolis Conference*, Rotterdam.

Ranger, T., Samad, Y. and Stuart, O. (eds) (1996) *Culture, Identity and Politics.* Ashgate, Aldershot.

Ratcliffe, P. (2004) *'Race', Ethnicity and Difference: Imagining the Inclusive Society.* Open University Press, Maidenhead.

Reichenberg, N.E. (2001) *Best Practices in Diversity Management.* Paper presented to United Nations Expert Group Meeting on Managing Diversity in the Civil Service, New York, May.

Rex, J. (2000) 'The Integration of Immigrants and Refugees in European Societies', in E. Appelt and M. Jarosch (eds) *Combating Racial Discrimination: Affirmative Action as a Model for Europe.* Berg, Oxford, 201–215.

Scheuer, S. (1992) 'Denmark: Return to Decentralisation', in A. Ferner and R. Hyman (eds) *Industrial Relations in the New Europe.* Basil Blackwell, Oxford, 168–197.

Schierup, C. (1993) *På Kulturens Slagmark: Mindretal og Størretal taler om Danmark.* Sydjysk Univesitet Centers forlag, Esbjerg.

Selznick, P. (1949) *TVA and the Grass Roots.* University of California Press, Berkeley.

Selznick, P. (1957) *Leadership in Administration.* Harper and Row, New York.

Shapiro, G. (2000) 'Employee involvement: opening the diversity Pandora's Box?', *Personnel Review* vol. 29 no. 3, 304–323.

Schnapper, D., Krief, P., Peignard, E. (2003) 'French Immigration and Integration Policy: A Complex Combination', in F. Heckmann and D. Schnapper (eds) *The Integration of Immigrants in European Societies: National Differences and Trends of Convergence.* Lucius and Lucius, Stuttgart, 15–44.

Simon, P. (2005) 'Measurement of racial discrimination: the policy use of statistics', in S. Mannila (ed.) *Data to Promote Equality* Finnish Ministry of Labour/European Commission, Helsinki, 77–100.

Simpson, A. and Stevenson, J. (1994) *Half a Chance, Still?* Nottingham and District Racial Equality Council, Nottingham.

Soininen M. and Graham, M. (1995) *Persuasion Contra Legislation. Preventing Racism at the Workplace: The Swedish national report.* European Foundation for the Improvement of Living and Working Conditions, Dublin.

Soininen. M. and Graham, M. (1997) *Case Studies of Good Practice for the Prevention of Racial Discrimination and Xenophobia and the Promotion of Equal Treatment at the Workplace: Sweden.* European Foundation for the Improvement of Living and Working Conditions, Dublin WP/97/47/EN.

Stewart, M. and Lindburgh, L. (1997) *Gaining from Diversity.* European Business Network for Social Cohesion, Brussels.

Sundin, E. (2000) 'Men are always suitable? A paper on the varying prerequisites for the implementation of diversity from a gender perspective' Proceedings of the conference *Workplace Diversity: A Research Perspective on Policy and Practice.* Brussels, June.

Taran, P. and Gächter, A. (2003) *Achieving Equality in Intercultural Workplaces: An Agenda for Action.* The Equality Authority, Dublin.

Taylor, P. (2000) 'Positive Action in the United Kingdom', in E. Appelt and M. Jarosch (eds) *Combating Racial Discrimination: Affirmative Action as a Model for Europe.* Berg, Oxford, 159–171.

Taylor, P., Powell, D. and Wrench, J. (1997) *The evaluation of anti-discrimination training activities in the United Kingdom.* International Labour Office, Geneva.

Thomas, R.R., Jr. (1990). 'From Affirmative Action to Affirming Diversity', *Harvard Business Review* March/April, 107–117.

Thomas, R.R., Jr. (1996) 'A Diversity Framework', in M.M. Chemers, S. Oskamp and M.A. Costanzo (eds) *Diversity in Organizations: New Perspectives for a Changing Workplace*, Sage, Thousand Oaks, California, 245–263.

Valtonen, K. (2001) 'Cracking monopoly: immigrants and employment in Finland', *Journal of Ethnic and Migration Studies* vol. 27 no. 3, 439–453.

Vertovec, S. and Wessendorf, S. (2005) *Migration and Cultural, Religious and Linguistic Diversity in Europe: An overview of issues and trends.* IMISCOE State of the Art Report, Cluster B6, Centre on Migration, Policy and Society, University of Oxford.

Virdee, S. (1997) *Case Studies of Good Practice for the Prevention of Racial Discrimination and Xenophobia and the Promotion of Equal Treatment at the Workplace: The UK.* European Foundation for the Improvement of Living and Working Conditions, Dublin, WP/97/48/EN.

Vuori, K. (1997) *Anti-discrimination training activities in Finland.* International Labour Office, Geneva.

Wentling, R.M. and Palma-Rivas, N. (1997a) *Diversity in the Workforce: A Literature Review.* Diversity in the Workforce Series Report no.1, MDS-934, National Center for Research in Vocational Education, University of California at Berkeley.

Wentling, R.M. and Palma-Rivas, N. (1997b) *Current Status and Future Trends of Diversity in the Workplace: Diversity Experts' Perspective.* Diversity in the Workforce Series Report no.2, MDS-1082, National Center for Research in Vocational Education, University of California at Berkeley.

Wentling, R.M. and Palma-Rivas, N. (1997c) *Current Status of Diversity Initiatives in Selected Multinational Corporations.* Diversity in the Workforce Series Report no.3, MDS-936, National Center for Research in Vocational Education, University of California at Berkeley.

Westin, C. (2000) *Settlement and Integration Policies towards Immigrants and their Descendants in Sweden.* International Labour Office, Geneva.

Williams, J. (1985) 'Redefining Institutional Racism', *Ethnic and Racial Studies*, vol. 8 no. 3, 323–348.

Williams, K.Y. and O'Reilly, C.A. III (1998) 'Demography and Diversity in Organisations: A review of 40 years of research', in B.M. Straw and L.L.Cummings (eds) *Research in Organizational Behaviour* vol. 20, Jai Pres, Connecticut, 77–140.

Williams, M.S. (2000) 'In Defence of Affirmative Action: North American Discourses for the European Context?', in E. Appelt and M. Jarosch (eds) *Combating Racial Discrimination: Affirmative Action as a Model for Europe.* Berg, Oxford.

Wise, L.R. (2000) 'Diversity Research: Eight things we know about the consequences of heterogeneity in the workplace', Paper presented at *Diversity Practice: Diversity Management and Integration – Ethnicity and Gender in Focus.* Work and Culture, Norrköping, November.

Wise, L.R. and Tschirhart, M. (2000) 'Examining Empirical Evidence on Diversity Effects: How Useful is Diversity Research for Public Sector Managers?', *Public Administration Review* vol. 60 no. 5, 386–395.

Woodward, J. (1965) *Industrial Organisation: Theory and Practice.* Oxford University Press, Oxford.

Wren, K. (2001) 'Cultural Racism: something rotten in the state of Denmark?', *Social and Cultural Geography* vol. 2 no. 2, 141–162.

Wren, K. and P. Boyle (2002) *Migration and Work-related Health in Europe – A Pilot Study.* Working Life Research in Europe no. 1, Arbetslivsinstitutet, Stockholm.

Wrench, J. (1987) 'Unequal Comrades: trade unions, equal opportunity and racism', in R. Jenkins and J. Solomos (eds) *Racism and Equal Opportunity Policies in the 1980s.* Cambridge University Press, Cambridge, 160–186.

Wrench, J. (1996) *Preventing Racism at the Workplace: A report on 16 European countries.* Office for Official Publications of the European Communities, Luxembourg.

Wrench, J. (1997a) *European Compendium of Good Practice for the Prevention of Racism at the Workplace.* Office for Official Publications of the European Communities, Luxembourg.

Wrench, J. (1997b) *Case Studies of Good Practice for the Prevention of Racial Discrimination and Xenophobia and the Promotion of Equal Treatment at the Workplace: Denmark.* European Foundation for the Improvement of Living and Working Conditions, Dublin WP/97/36/EN.

Wrench, J. (1998) *The EU, Ethnic Minorities and Migrants at the Workplace.* European Dossier Series, Kogan Page, London.

Wrench, J. (2000) *Trade unions, immigrants and ethnic minorities in Europe: Report on the Danish national project.* European Social Fund 'INTEGRA' Project no. I 1997 DK 508, Unpublished report, University of Southern Denmark, Esbjerg.

Wrench, J. (2001) 'Anti-discrimination training at the workplace in Europe: The application of an international typology', in M. Essemyr (ed.) *Diversity in Work Organisations.* National Institute for Working Life, Stockholm, 119–152.

Wrench, J. (2004) *Breakthroughs and Blind Spots: Trade union responses to immigrants and ethnic minorities in Denmark and the UK.* Fafo, Oslo.

Wrench, J. and Taylor, P. (1993) *A Research Manual on the Evaluation of Anti-Discrimination Training Activities.* International Labour Office, Geneva.

Zarrehparvar, M. and Hildebrandt, S. (2005) 'Discrimination in Denmark' in S. Nour and L.N. Thisted (eds) *Diversity in the workplace: When we are equal but not the same.* Børsens Forlag, Copenhagen, 45–70.

Zegers de Beijl, R. (ed.) (2000) *Documenting Discrimination against Migrant Workers in the Labour Market: A comparative study of four European countries.* International Labour Office, Geneva.

Index